T0332135

# crucial
## influence

# crucial influence

## THIRD EDITION

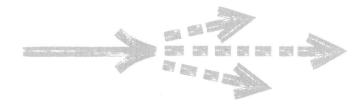

## LEADERSHIP SKILLS TO CREATE
## LASTING BEHAVIOR CHANGE

JOSEPH GRENNY • KERRY PATTERSON • DAVID MAXFIELD
RON McMILLAN • AL SWITZLER

Mc
Graw
Hill

NEW YORK   CHICAGO   SAN FRANCISCO   ATHENS   LONDON
MADRID   MEXICO CITY   MILAN   NEW DELHI
SINGAPORE   SYDNEY   TORONTO

1  2  3  4  5  6  7  8  9    LCR    28  27  26  25  24  23

ISBN        978-1-265-04965-2 (paperback)
MHID           1-265-04965-3 (paperback)

ISBN        978-1-265-05119-8 (hardcover)
MHID           1-265-05119-4 (hardcover)

e-ISBN      978-1-265-05018-4
e-MHID         1-265-05018-X

McGraw Hill books are available at special quantity discounts to use as premiums and sales promotions or for use in corporate training programs. To contact a representative, please visit the Contact Us pages at www.mhprofessional.com.

McGraw Hill is committed to making our products accessible to all learners. To learn more about the available support and accommodations we offer, please contact us at accessibility@mheducation.com. We also participate in the Access Text Network (www.accesstext.org), and ATN members may submit requests through ATN.

The first two editions of this book were published under the title *Influencer.*

We dedicate this book
to great leaders everywhere—
to those who have not only added to
an ever-growing knowledge
of how people change
but also restored hope,
inspired action, and made it possible
for each of us to amplify our influence
to change the world for good.

Along with this collective dedication,
we add our love and gratitude
for one leader in particular.
Our friend, coauthor, and colleague,
Kerry Patterson (1946–2022),
dedicated his life to bettering
the lives of others.
We, therefore, dedicate this expression
of his hard-earned wisdom to him.

# CONTENTS

# Contents

# ACKNOWLEDGMENTS

We are deeply grateful to many who have helped us throughout the years in our research, teaching, testing, and learning.

First, our appreciation to our families for your influence on us. Thanks for the love and support that has changed us, inspired us, and enabled us. Thank you particularly for your sacrifice and patience when we were far from home—or at home, but overly focused, head down over a keyboard.

Second, thanks to our colleagues, associates, and team members at Crucial Learning who help in hundreds of ways—working to achieve our mission, serving customers, training the skills to help change lives, and supporting one another with care, loyalty, and competence. To all, we say thanks. A special thanks to Bruce Bennett, a gifted organizational expert who helped conceive the model of the six sources of influence.

Third, a special thanks to Chase McMillan, Mindy Waite, and Mary McChesney, whose love of, belief in, and intrepid effort for this project made it far more than it would otherwise be. Chase maneuvered us into many of the most important case studies in this book. Mindy labored meticulously to bring clarity, simplicity, and beauty to the text. And Mary gave inspired vision and project leadership to the entire effort. Much of what is good in the present book is a credit to these three.

And fourth, we're overwhelmingly grateful to our friends and partners across the planet who have turned these ideas from an interesting read into a global force for positive change. We are inspired by the soul and skill they bring to our cooperative effort.

# PART I

## HOW THE WORLD WORKS—AND HOW TO CHANGE IT

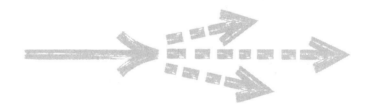

# 1

# LEADERSHIP
# IS INFLUENCE

---

*Influence is the common need embedded in almost everything
we care about. If it involves people, it's an influence problem.*

---

It wasn't the most harrowing research junket we had ever taken. Nothing like earlier adventures in our influence research to some of the more dangerous parts of the world. No threat of deadly parasites, no fear of being kidnapped, no wrangling with corrupt politicians.

This time, our research took us to New York City to one of the Big Apple's finest restaurants where, as part of our demanding research regime, we'd be tossing back tasty appetizers while chatting with a brilliant restaurateur. (It was a tough job, but someone had to do it.) This was all part of an ongoing project to discover how remarkable leaders leverage thoughtful influence of human behavior to achieve big results.

The person we visited on this particular day was Danny Meyer. Danny earned our attention by gaining top ratings on most major customer review sites for a diverse group of restaurants—for *decades*. You might suspect that his continued success results from hiring better people, designing more beautiful spaces, buying better ingredients, or crafting better dishes. But Meyer is convinced these have little to do with their success. He assures us that his competitors hire from the same labor pool, shop with the same vendors, and produce similarly delicious food. What distinguishes Union Square Hospitality Group restaurants, according to Danny Meyer, is not places and products; it is behavior. Danny's hallmark capacity is his ability to influence 1,500 employees to consistently create extraordinary experiences for their 100,000 daily guests.

Danny Meyer: "My job is to influence 1,500 people
to create special experiences for 100,000 customers every day."

For example, a woman frantically rushed through the entrance of Gramercy Tavern, one of Danny's establishments located in the Flatiron District of Manhattan. The potential diner was distraught because she had left her purse in the taxi that dropped her off. The blood drained from the woman's face as she realized that not only would she probably never see her purse again, but she also had no way to pay for the meal for the clients she was hosting.

An employee (let's call him Carlo) noticed the stranger's look of panic, learned of her problem, and urged her to relax and join her party—who were already seated and waiting for her.

"Don't worry about paying," Carlo comforted her. "We'll settle up some other time. For now, please enjoy yourself. In the meantime, what is your phone number?"

Surmising that the frantic customer had likely left her phone in her purse, Carlo asked a colleague to repeatedly call the number. Thirty minutes later when the taxi driver finally heard the ring and answered the call, he was many miles north in the Bronx. Carlo then flashed the Batman signal onto the side of a building to summon the Caped Crusader . . .

OK, the Batman thing isn't true, . . . but what Carlo did do was still quite heroic. He arranged to meet the taxi halfway between the Gramercy Tavern and the Bronx. He paid the driver for his trouble, retrieved the purse, and presented it to the woman just as she finished her lunch. That night she renamed her beloved corgi "Carlo."

What makes this incident remarkable is not just that it happened at all, but that similar actions routinely occur in each of Danny's restaurants. Employees go above and beyond to create an unparalleled customer experience. Danny sets himself apart from 20,000 other New York restaurateurs with the way he uses *influence*. Danny's staff members behave markedly differently from your average restaurant employee because of Danny's systematic and intentional actions aimed at influencing very specific behavior.

That's why we traveled to New York. We went to study true leadership.

## LEADERSHIP IS INTENTIONAL INFLUENCE

Now, let's be clear. This isn't a book about customer service. Likewise, when we later visit a man in Salt Lake City who has helped thousands of felons turn their lives around, we won't be studying criminal psychology. And when we look at efforts aimed at eradicating diseases, improving patient safety, reducing violence against women, or making virtual workforces work, our interest won't be in exploring these topics either.

What we *will* be doing is looking for the common thread that connects all successful leaders—no matter the objective or the setting. We'll explore a common set of principles and skills that can help you achieve things that can only be accomplished by changing human behavior. We'll be studying *influence.*

At the end of the day, *leadership is intentional influence.* If behavior isn't changing, you aren't leading.

Despite what some have suggested in past decades, leadership isn't simply about crafting inspiring visions or challenging the status quo. Neither is it about coming up with a breakthrough product or architecting detailed business growth plans. A solitary genius sitting in a tower all alone can do those things.

Leadership is about mobilizing *others* to achieve the vision, challenge the status quo, build breakthrough products, and execute flawlessly on lofty plans. Leadership is the human process of cooperative achievement. True leaders possess the repeatable capacity to influence rapid, profound, and sustainable behavior change to produce valued results.

Now, as you hear the word *influence*, you might think that we're referring to the less impressive and more suspicious tool called *persuasion.* We're not. This book is not about solving problems or hitting new targets by applying the right combination of verbal tricks. If you're looking to reach rather modest goals by stealthily exerting your will over others, this book is not for you. Likewise, the term *influencer* these days has come to be more a measure of online popularity than the capacity to lead meaningful change. You can't open a car door these days without the risk of hitting a self-appointed "influencer." Some of these folks might be good at getting attention, but a precious few have demonstrated the capacity to systematically engage all the elements of influence required to help people change deeply embedded behaviors to dramatically improve their lives. As we'll see, *influence* is about far more than just being an *influencer*. To that end, we've made the important decision to change the title of the book in this third edition from *Influencer* to *Crucial Influence*.

This book has much loftier and more enduring goals, requiring much stronger tools. It explores how to achieve better results everywhere—from a gold mine in Ghana to a family in Geneva to a software team in Guangzhou—by changing entrenched human habits.

We'll examine in detail 'why people do what they do and what it takes to help them act differently. Whether you're stopping AIDS or starting a company safety program, the key to success has little to do with pep talks, bribes, or your expert use of social media. Instead, success relies on deploying a critical mass of the sources of influence that shape all human behavior.

## A Leader Who Influenced Change

For example, after years of missed deadlines and buggy code from teams that produce large, complex software systems, Rich Sheridan, CEO of Menlo Innovations, began scrupulously studying the behaviors behind the blunders. The search began with an epiphany: "I needed to think less about the code and more about the humans that create the code."

Sheridan soon concluded that the key to consistent high-quality performance was influencing his employees to practice two *vital behaviors*: (1) admit when they have problems, and (2) speak up immediately when they won't meet a deadline. He found that when sprawling teams of software engineers did these two things consistently, products got completed correctly and on time.

His next problem was figuring out how to get dozens, and sometimes hundreds of people to do these two things.

His challenge was that your typical human is more willing to donate a kidney than to admit failure. No simple speech or manipulative technique will overcome the overwhelming inducements toward silence that most employees experience in the workplace.

By carefully working to influence these behaviors with the strategy we'll share in this book, Sheridan was able to change his team's behavior and overcome Menlo's quality control concerns.

## Change Requires Influence

Sheridan's record of accomplishment at Menlo Innovations is a testament to true leadership. He and his team have developed a culture around these two behaviors that results in unmatched on-time, on-budget, on-spec performance. And they did so using precisely the same principles of influence that Danny Meyer uses to inspire first-class hospitality.

Throughout this book, we'll explore influence strategies from leaders like Rich and Danny who are successful because they understand that *leadership is intentional influence*. They have systematic and repeatable ways of thinking about why people do what they do and what it takes to help them change. They think about influencing behavior, talk about it, and practice it, and all of them have created remarkable changes in domains where failure has been the norm—often for decades.

Now, you may not work in a software development firm or a restaurant, but there's a good chance that human beings are involved with some of the things that challenge you the most.

Perhaps you'd like to help a troubled son who has just returned from his third drug rehab. You may be baffled about how to reduce turnover in your call center, improve customer service in your government office, or raise graduation rates in your high school. One of the best ways to get better at addressing each of these challenges is to get better at influence. Influence is the common need embedded in almost everything we care about. If it involves people, it's an influence problem.

> *Wondering how you can make change happen? Read our study* How to 10X Your Influence *and learn how the Crucial Influence model can increase your odds of success tenfold. Read it at CrucialInfluence.com.*

## WHY WE LACK INFLUENCE

Learning how to motivate and enable others to change their actions may be the most important skill you'll ever acquire. Given the value of knowing how to help other people act differently, you'd think that at every backyard barbecue or office party you could find someone who is an expert in influence. In fact, you'd think we'd be so consumed with the topic of influence that our children would collect influence trading cards, complete with pictures of world-class leaders. As a result of all this study and passion, we would speak a unique language, carry a full array of models, and master a specialized set of skills for both enabling and encouraging others to change their behavior.

Of course, none of this is true. Most of us can't verbalize our personal theory of influence or even recognize that as leaders we need one! That's why few of us can remember the last time we saw a change attempt conducted at our place of work yield anything more than the occasional T-shirt or mug emblazoned with the name of the effort. And we're in good company. Our review of the past 30 years of change literature reveals that fewer than one in eight workplace change efforts produce anything other than cynicism.

We're equally challenged at home. For instance, every year we spend billions on diets and lose little more than our money. Fewer than 10 percent of us succeed when we set out to change our excessive spending, inadequate exercise, and other unhelpful habits.

Communities fare no better. Two-thirds of the felons released from our "correctional" system return within three years—completely uncorrected—while having earned an advanced degree in crime. Stopping the spread of pandemics requires people to change habits, yet millions of individuals are infected every year because we humans are bad at changing habits.

As a result of all of these failed influence efforts and unfulfilled dreams, most of us grow impatient. We ask, "Why aren't people doing what they should be doing, and why can't I get them to change?" Eventually, we settle on the strategy recommended by essayist David Sedaris: "I haven't got the slightest idea how to change people, but still I keep a long list of prospective candidates just in case I should ever figure it out."[1]

But there *are* real leaders out there.

## FINDING INFLUENCERS

To expand our understanding of influence and the central role influence skills play in what matters most to us in life, we began a systematic study of what works. This ongoing research took three forms: the literature, the leaders, and the learners.

### The Literature

As most researchers do, we began by reading. Our research team pored over more than 17,000 articles and books to find scholars and practitioners who have mastered various aspects of influence. From these, we identified those who had succeeded at influencing rapid, profound, and sustainable changes in ways that most of the world thinks are impossible.

## The Leaders

Next, we tracked down these rare individuals and closely examined their work. For instance, we traveled to Thailand to study the work of Wiwat Rojanapithayakorn, who saved over 5 million Thai citizens from contracting HIV/AIDS. While he had little to no organizational power as he began his campaign, he found a way to influence the behavior of his 60 million fellow Thai citizens. Years after he finished this work, we caught up again in Bangkok. Over dinner, about as casually as you'd mention you had downloaded a new app, he reported that his government asked him to help 9 million people stop smoking in the next five years. And at the time of writing, he was on track to finish a couple of years early. The most effective leaders don't stumble into success; they develop repeatable ways of systematically influencing lasting change.

Dr. Wiwat Rojanapithayakorn was director of Thailand's Center for the Prevention and Control of AIDS.

Other remarkable leaders we'll talk about in this book who are effecting change include:

- Martha Swai, an influencer in Tanzania, who helped reduce spousal abuse across the entire nation through the use of, of all things, a unique kind of radio program.
- Dain Hancock, president of Lockheed Martin Aeronautics, who influenced remarkable behavior change across a cynical and resistant 13,000-person workforce, helping him land a $1 trillion contract.
- Antanas Mockus, a math-professor-turned-mayor in Bogotá, Colombia, who, during a terrible water shortage, reduced water use by 40 percent among his constituents in a matter of months.

In Chapter 3 see how Martha Swai used a story to change a nation.

We studied other notable leaders who helped longtime felons become productive citizens, saved thousands from dying from hospital errors, and lifted millions out of poverty—to name but a few of their accomplishments. And it turned out every one of these leaders had done it in precisely the same way. All used the same influence principles we are about to share.

## The Learners

It's one thing to *explain* success in retrospect. It's another to repeatedly create it. Our confidence in the value of the leadership skills you're about to study has increased over the decades since this book was first published. We've watched thousands of parents, supervisors, managers, and executives like you learn these skills and put them into practice. A small sampling of the kind of rapid and remarkable changes they've led include:

- The owner of Gallery Furniture in Houston, Texas, dramatically reduced damage happening during deliveries.
- The CEO of telecom giant MTN increased innovation in a workforce spanning Africa and the Middle East.
- A senior manager at the biotechnology firm, Genentech, improved decisions by involving more stakeholders without creating wasteful delays.
- A director at Intermountain Healthcare turned customer service skills into consistent habits across a large hospital.

In Chapter 2, Laura Grams and Lisa Doyle at HCA Healthcare
discover the behaviors that are vital to retaining and engaging nurses.

- VPs of HR and Learning at HCA Healthcare influenced nursing retention during periods of high turnover.
- An eBay executive fostered greater collaboration between siloed teams.
- A Willow Creek Food Pantry manager made it safer and less stressful for patrons to use their services.
- State Farm leaders dramatically increased cross-selling success.
- Leaders at Fundación Paraguaya helped thousands in need increase their household income.
- A PricewaterhouseCoopers (PwC) executive increased retention and promotion of underrepresented groups in senior positions.
- A group of Certified Financial Planners helped at-risk clients change their spending habits during a major recession.
- Newmont Mining site managers saved lives by increasing safety compliance.
- The Pakistani superintendent of police stemmed corruption and reduced traffic fatalities by 60 percent.
- MoneyGram HR managers influenced employees to resolve more problems at the peer level before escalating them.
- Pizza Hut managers improved team responses to crowded stores, product failures, upset customers, and equipment problems.
- Leaders at KIPP schools increased principal retention from 2.3 years to 4.7 years.

We'll go into detail on some of these campaigns in the book, but we claim no ownership of the ideas we will share. We hope we have added value by organizing them in a portable and practical way for you. But the wisdom they contain is the product of a century of research by a legion of intrepid social scientists and evidence produced by countless leaders.

Our goal is to help you see that in almost every vital role you play, influence is an essential competence. We are confident that the time you'll invest in studying what comes next will be well rewarded as you learn to better understand why those you care most about do what they do, and more importantly, how to help them change.

# 2

# THE THREE KEYS
# TO INFLUENCE

---

*When you understand how the world works,*
*you're in a better position to change it.*

---

There are three things effective leaders do better than the rest of us. All three show a more effective way of approaching influence. Our goal in this book is to show you a better way of thinking about every influence challenge in your life.

Before we get to the three keys, you need to know that everyone has a theory of influence. Even if you don't think you do, you do! This theory shows up every time you answer two questions:

1. Why are they doing *that*?
2. How can I help them do *this* instead?

You answer these questions all the time. Say you're driving on the freeway and the person in front of you is going 15 mph (24 kph) below the speed limit. You may not realize it, but in the nanoseconds between tapping on your brakes and muttering words of "encouragement" directed at the other driver, you answered the question, "Why are they driving so slowly?" And the way you answered that question drew from a theory you carry about why *everyone* does what they do.

When your spouse is tardy to commitments, when a fast-food employee forgets to put french fries in your bag, and when your boss fails to support your promotion, you reflexively generate an answer to the "why" question.

Your influence theory also determines how you'll try to get others to change. We all have influence biases—tactics we default to when people aren't behaving the way we want them to—whether it's reasoning, bargaining, nagging, guilt-tripping, or sermonizing. Let's begin our effort to improve the way we think about influence by sharing how the remarkable leaders we've studied answer these two questions. In fact, let's up the ante. Let's talk first not just about the handful of people you'd like to influence, let's talk about the whole planet. In the next few paragraphs, we'll offer a better way of thinking about *how the world works* and *how to change the world.* Then we'll apply these insights to the two questions above.

## HOW THE WORLD WORKS, AND HOW TO CHANGE IT

Look at the following model. A helpful way to think about the way the world works is to move from left to right along this model. On the left, you see what looks like a six-pane window labeled "Six Sources of Influence." We'll detail these later, but for now, we suggest that there are six different kinds of influence that shape our choices.

Moving to the right, you see a hamster wheel labeled "Vital Behaviors." The idea is that when the six sources of influence remain stable over time, they help us make choices and shape our behaviors. These behaviors produce "Results" ( far right)—both good and bad.

Crucial Influence® Model

For example, let's say you work in a hospital. For a variety of reasons (six sources of influence), many of your doctors and nurses fail to follow good hand-hygiene practices. If those reasons don't change, these sloppy practices will harden into organizational norms (bad hygiene habits). And those bad habits will create consequences (results), like an increase in hospital-acquired infections. That's how the world works.

Hospital Hand-Hygiene Example

Now that you understand how the world works, you're in a better position to change it. The way you change the world using this model is from *right to left*. That's right, the best leaders tackle influence challenges in the opposite direction from how the world typically operates. They use three skills that build on each other to move from right to left:

1.  First, focus on *results*. Great leaders are better at articulating what they want to achieve and how they will measure it.

2. Second, identify a small handful of *vital behaviors*. These are the specific behavioral changes needed to disproportionately improve results.

3. Third, engage all *six sources of influence* to support your vital behaviors.

How to Change the World

In this chapter, we'll help you understand why these three disciplines are crucial to effective influence. We'll elaborate on *results* and *vital behaviors* and leave the rest of the book to help you think and act more effectively by engaging all six sources of influence.

## KEY 1: FOCUS AND MEASURE

To shine a light on this first influence key, we'll meet with Dr. Donald Hopkins in Atlanta, Georgia. Dr. Hopkins is a physician and the former vice president of healthcare programs at The Carter Center. He attracted our attention by taking on one of the most daunting influence challenges in history. His goal is to eradicate a horrendous global disease . . . without finding a cure.

To remind himself of his goal, Dr. Hopkins keeps a specimen of his foe on his desk in a jar of formaldehyde. If his enemy could stand, she would be three feet tall. But she has no skeletal system. She's a worm. More specifically, she's a Guinea worm.

Helping individuals who have contracted Guinea worm disease is an enormous challenge because once someone has it, it will inevitably run its miserable course through the host's body. Medical science offers no hope of relief. None. There are no medicines, surgeries, or magical techniques. Once a person has the worm, it will cause havoc every single time. Given that medical science had little to offer, Dr. Hopkins turned to social science.

When Dr. Hopkins came on the scene, over 3 million people in 23,000 remote villages in 20 countries were contracting Guinea worm disease every year. The disease begins when villagers get a little more in their drink of water than they bargained for. Hiding within the fetid ponds that many use as a water source lie the Guinea worm larvae.

When swallowed, the larvae hatch into worms inside the host's body, then slowly burrow back out by whatever route they choose, through the muscle and skin on an arm, a leg—well, you can imagine the other options.

This journey causes such enormous pain and suffering that the host eventually rushes to the nearest water source and plunges the emerging worm into the water to find a moment of relief. At this point, the worm ejects thousands of eggs into the pond—guaranteeing next year's crop of Guinea worms—when the awful process begins again as it has for thousands of years.

Dr. Hopkins took an interest in the Guinea worm because he concluded that it could literally be eradicated from the planet. All he had to do, he told us matter-of-factly, was change the behavior of 120 million people spread over 10 million square miles.

How would you approach this kind of problem? With a team of two dozen people and a few million dollars in the budget, how could you even *think* about getting millions of strangers to change?

Dr. Hopkins (like all the leaders we studied) knows how to think about these kinds of problems and develop repeatable and effective strategies to solve them.

The first thing effective leaders do is *focus and measure.* They clearly articulate the goal they're trying to achieve. They know that fuzzy objectives hinder influence and clear, consistent, and meaningful measures are the foundation of influence.

Dr. Hopkins told us that job one was to create a reporting system in affected countries to get accurate information about both the prevalence of infection and the progress of the interventions they would attempt. "Measurement isn't just about tracking results," he said. "It's also about motivating action."

With a boyish grin he showed us one of his favorite progress reports. It was a graphic of an oval racetrack with the faces of the heads of state of various Guinea-worm-affected countries. He described a moment when he met with one president who had lost focus on Guinea worm eradication efforts. "I pulled out a stack of reports, but the only one he wanted to see was the racetrack that showed him lagging far behind two neighboring countries. Everything changed after that meeting."

Effective measurement drives attention, motivation, and learning. Less effective leaders measure out of habit or compliance. The things they measure are simply inherited norms or demands from outside stakeholders. True leaders know that the only substantive reason to measure anything is to drive behavior.

The way you know if you're measuring the right things in the right way is by asking, "How does this measure influence behavior?"

Of the hundreds of influence attempts we've studied over the years, the vast majority of them fail at the outset by neglecting this first key. Unsuccessful leaders make one of two early mistakes that undermine their influence: they fail to fully define desired results, or they don't take the right kinds of measurements.

## Failing to Define Desired Results

You'd think that if people got one only thing right when trying to create a change, it would be defining their objective. Their objective, after all, is the voice that calls out for change in the first place. "We have really poor customer service." "Our inner-city kids need help." "Our quality is mediocre, and we want to be the best."

The goals associated with each of these cries for change seem obvious. Leaders need to improve customer service, help inner-city kids, and push quality to new heights. Such goal statements sound good, but they are too vague to exert any influence. "Improving customer service" could be interpreted as everything from answering the phone by the second ring to giving customers a free hamster with every purchase over $50.

To see how top leaders set clear and measurable goals, consider the near-legendary work of Dr. Don Berwick, the former CEO of the Institute for Healthcare Improvement (IHI).

Despite IHI's diminutive size and Berwick's complete lack of position power in the $4 trillion US healthcare industry, he is universally described as one of the most influential people in the field and a fine example of making strong use of clear and compelling goals. In 2004, he was tasked with reducing deaths due to medical errors.

"I think it's unacceptable," Berwick told us, "that the sixth leading cause of death in the United States is healthcare. We inadvertently kill the equivalent of a jumbo jet filled with passengers every day of the year. We know how it happens, and we know how to avoid it. The challenge is influencing people to stop it from happening."

In December of that year, Berwick stood in front of a group of thousands of healthcare professionals and issued an audacious challenge by setting a clear and compelling goal: "I think we should save 100,000 lives from medical errors. I think we should do it by 18 months from today." Pause. "By 9 a.m."

The success of the 100,000 Lives Campaign is now in the record books.

How did Berwick and his team accomplish such a feat? He started with a clearly defined goal. He and his team weren't just going to "try to reduce medical errors." They weren't going to "improve safety." They weren't going to save an impressive number of lives "as soon as they could." They were going to save 100,000 lives from medical errors by 9 a.m. of June 14 of the next year.

There's no room for misinterpretation here. You're saving lives, not simply changing numbers on a chart. And you know exactly how many and by when. We'll learn a bit more later about how Berwick led the ultimate success of this effort, but none of those subsequent tactics would have influenced change without the foundation of this first key.

Clear goals aimed at a meaningful target can have an enormous impact on behavior because they engage more than simply the brain. They also engage the heart. Research reveals that a clear and challenging goal causes the blood to pump more rapidly, the brain to fire, and the muscles to engage. However, when goals are vague, no such effects take place.[1]

We saw firsthand what happens when a leader clearly defines the objective. This time we visited with Martín Burt who started Fundación Paraguaya more than 35 years ago. Initially, his goal was to provide Paraguay's poor with access to credit as a means of helping them climb out of poverty. Unfortunately, after spending 25 years trying to meet that goal, Burt became concerned that many people were getting access to credit, but too few were emerging from poverty.

As Burt and his leadership team reassessed their goal, they made a stunning change. No longer would they focus on how many loans they processed (a somewhat uncompelling goal). Instead, they announced the following: beginning in April 2011, "Our goal is to help 5,000 poor families to earn $5 per day per person [the national poverty line] or more before the end of the year."

Leaders of Fundación Paraguaya pivoted an entire organization
in record time beginning with resetting the way they measured success.

The effect of providing this clear, compelling, and time-bound target was immediate. It started a whole chain of events that virtually reshaped the organization. It influenced the way people saw their jobs. It influenced the skills loan officers would need to work with clients. It influenced a million conversations that happened between Fundación Paraguaya employees and their clients over the next eight months. And best of all, it generated enormous pride when on December 31, 2011, Burt announced that over *6,000* families had achieved this goal. And it all started with a clear, compelling goal and a meaningful way to measure it—the first key to influence.

Great leaders don't merely start their change efforts with their ultimate results in mind. They take care to craft their goals into a clear and compelling *results statement* that provides focus and motivation to teams, organizations, and even whole countries to rally around a compelling cause.

## Making Measurement Mistakes

Change efforts are often undermined by three common measurement mistakes. Either leaders take no measures, they measure something too distant to be motivating, or their measures are too infrequent to sustain attention.

## Failure to Take Measures

The most obvious and surprisingly common measurement mistake is not measuring at all. People often leave out this step for several reasons:

- They think they already have a firm grasp on the results they care about. But their conclusions are based on anecdotal evidence and gut impressions rather than reliable measures.
- They're naive about influence. They don't understand what it takes to engage human attention and motivation.
- They're avoiding accountability—for example, business leaders who shy away from setting aggressive growth targets that will be tracked publicly, or drug rehab providers who protest legislation that would require them to report long-term sobriety rates for those paying for their pricey services.
- It's just not a priority. Creating influential measures takes work. We've heard countless arguments such as, "We're too busy and resource-constrained to put effort into measurement."

At the end of the day, measurement is the truest test of our motives. Why should anyone trust the sincerity of your commitment to your goal if you aren't willing to put a stake in the ground and test whether you've delighted customers, saved lives, or increased revenues? A lack of measures can be evidence of a lack of real commitment.

## Measuring Something Too Distant

Let's return to the hospital where nurses and doctors are inadvertently passing germs from patient to patient due to poor hand hygiene. The CEO announces an inspiring *result*: Within twelve months, we will achieve a sustainable record of zero incidents of hospital-acquired infections.

This result is clear and motivating. But measuring infections alone might not generate sufficient motivation for frontline workers who feel too distant from the aspiration. You'll need to measure something close enough to them that they feel useful in contributing to the result.

People who feel no control have no sense of connection. So it's crucial to include a measure that will demonstrate meaningful progress toward the goal for everyone involved. For example, you might develop a way of tracking hand-hygiene compliance unit by unit within the hospital.

We once consulted with the US Army in their efforts to reduce sexual assault within the military. When we started, their sole measure was total reported assaults across the entire army. Few leaders up and down the chain felt any accountability or connection to the numbers. An Army captain with a company of a few dozen soldiers might have zero "reported assaults" but still be failing to create the right climate to keep their soldiers safe.

We urged Army leadership to create a closer, more controllable and motivating measure. We suggested they find a variable that would be highly predictive of reduced assaults, but within the control of lower-level officers. Meaningful variables can include changes in beliefs, attitudes, or behaviors that predict improvement in the results you're after. We encouraged them to consider:

- What beliefs, attitudes, or behaviors could you measure . . .
- that are largely influenced by the immediate commander . . . (closer)
- and would dramatically predict or prevent the result you care about (more motivating)?

After careful deliberation, they determined to hold every commander from captain upward accountable for ensuring that everyone they lead can say two things:

1. If I were sexually assaulted or harassed, I would report it with full confidence it would be properly investigated.
2. If I were at risk of being assaulted or harassed, I have full confidence my battle buddies would intervene to stop it.

Find a measure close enough to those you need to influence that they feel able and motivated to do something about it.

## Measurement Is Too Infrequent

Finally, an influential measure must be taken frequently enough to sustain attention. Imagine going to a sporting event where the score was revealed only at the end. In all likelihood, not only would the fans head for the exits, but the players would too. Measurement must both sustain attention and inform action. In other words, it must keep the mission front of mind while also providing feedback to your key players about whether their influence strategy is working.

In a world awash with data, the measures that get attention are the ones that are refreshed regularly. In a sense, they gamify the audacious objective you're working to achieve. Successful games generate a satisfying sense of mastery by offering the possibility of frequent score increases.

A group of cardiac researchers once lamented to the legendary psychologist Albert Bandura that too few patients consistently took their heart medication. Bandura suggested they send patients home with an inexpensive monitor with which they could test their blood pressure twice a day. As patients saw progress corresponding to their medication compliance, compliance soared. The measure both sustained the patients' attention and provided feedback about their actions. You must do the same.

This is why so few efforts to change organizational culture work. Leaders often refuse to take "soft measures" more often than every year or so. At the same time, managers get updates on budgets, sales, or production weekly or monthly. In that world, guess how much leadership attention culture change gets? Zippo. You'll get a week or two of self-flagellation when the annual survey is updated, while managers wait confidently for the focus to shift predictably to the higher-frequency metrics.

*A measure won't drive behavior if it doesn't maintain attention. And it won't maintain attention if it's rarely assessed*—especially if other measures are taken and discussed more frequently.

For example, what do you think would happen if our friend Danny Meyer measured restaurant revenues daily but customer experience only annually? Revenue would drive management attention, and customer experience would get a ritualized yearly review—as is the case in most of Danny's competitors.

Leaders often complain that it takes as much effort to measure an influence campaign as it does to deploy the campaign itself. And within this complaint lies the real problem. Leaders assume measurement is separate from influence. It isn't. Measurement is influence.

The first step in any effective influence strategy is to articulate a clear and compelling statement of the results you want and to develop a close, controllable, and frequent method of measuring progress.

## KEY 2: FIND VITAL BEHAVIORS

Every year more than 3,000 Americans drown, many of them in public pools. This problem remained unchanged for decades until a team of leaders from the YMCA and Redwoods Insurance got serious about influence. It wasn't long before they had reduced the portion of these 3,000 deaths that happened at YMCA pools by two-thirds.

How did they do it? They studied tragedies and successes until they found one vital (high-leverage) behavior that made the difference. They discovered that traditional lifeguards were spending much of their time greeting members, adjusting swim lanes, picking up kickboards, and testing pool chemicals. (Doesn't sound much like *life-guarding*, does it?)

However, when lifeguards do *10-10 scanning*, drowning rates drop immediately. Each lifeguard scans their section of the pool every 10 seconds, then offers assistance to anyone who *might* be in trouble within 10 seconds. Simple. And it yields incredibly high leverage.

Redwoods Insurance worked with YMCAs across the world to help spare hundreds of families from devastating loss of life by identifying and implementing this one *vital behavior* that made all the difference.

If you're influencing others, their behavior should be changing. True influence results in new behavior. It may seem strange that we need to emphasize this, but the truth is many leaders turn leadership into a mystical smoke about "changing hearts and minds."

Yes, to influence people's behavior, you'll need to influence the way they feel and the way they think. But those are means to an end, not the end itself. The end you're after is for some human being to vote, wash their hands, smile sincerely at a customer, or speak up about safety risks. You want new habits, not just new feelings.

Thus, the second key to influence is to clearly articulate the new behaviors you believe will disproportionately affect the results you want to achieve. We call these *vital behaviors*.

It turns out that even with very complex problems, often just one or two behaviors produce the greatest amount of change. Take for example the remarkable influence of The Other Side Academy in Salt Lake City, Utah, USA.[2]

Dave Durocher has one of the most unique employee populations in the world. As executive director of The Other Side Academy, he leads some of the most respected businesses in the region. In fact, in 2017, he and his colleagues won the prestigious Ernst and Young Entrepreneur of the Year award for their leadership of The Other Side Movers, the top-rated moving company in the state for many years running.

Leaders of The Other Side Academy have found two vital behaviors that help those with deeply troubled lives achieve profound change.

The win was surprising because not only have Dave's 200 team members been arrested an average of 25 times each, but Dave himself was incarcerated for over 20 years prior to joining the Academy. It took a swarm of police helicopters and SWAT specialists to capture him just over a decade ago to face another 22 years in prison.

After lengthy pleading, a judge told him that if he stayed two full years at a program called Delancey Street (a legendary program the Academy is modeled after), he would be forgiven of his outstanding sentence. In the end, he stayed eight years and became one of the most impressive leaders we've ever met.

The Other Side Academy is a three-to-four-year, no-cost, self-supporting academy for those with deeply broken lives. Its goal is to help students achieve "whole-person change." Current students include a woman named Tiffany who lived under a bridge for most of her younger years. Her mother first introduced her to meth when she was 11 years old. She grew up violent, addicted, and aimless.

After an arrest for an especially heinous crime, Tiffany heard about The Other Side Academy. Her judge agreed that if she could complete the rigorous life-skills experience at the Academy she would be forgiven of her outstanding sentence.

Roughly 80 percent of students come to The Other Side Academy as an alternative to additional incarceration. If the current student population was not at the Academy, they would instead be collectively serving over 1,000 years of prison or jail time. Tiffany's colleagues include a man arrested for a string of interstate robberies, a gang member facing multiple five-to-life sentences, and a generous number of former drug dealers.

This might seem like a risky employee pool for a moving company. But take a moment sometime to examine online reviews of The Other Side Movers, and you'll think people are describing a visit to a high-end spa. Hundreds of five-star reviews tout the kindness, integrity, speed, and professionalism of students.

Although students at the Academy often hail from rival gangs, there has never been an act of violence between students. While almost all of the students were hardcore heroin, crack, or meth users the day before they arrived, probation and parole officials who check students every month have never reported a dirty drug test. And when city officials asked neighbors if they were concerned about a large concentration of felons moving into their neighborhood, all 55 of those who turned out to make public comments rhapsodized about what wonderful citizens they are.

How does Durocher run world-class enterprises that generate the millions needed to support the students year after year with a population most would consider castoffs? A key to the success of The Other Side Academy is a relentless focus on two vital behaviors.

Durocher says, "Our problem was never that we were drug addicts. Our problem is that over time we became liars, thieves, cheats, manipulators, and narcissists. We either never had—or lost—the character required to live a life of integrity, accountability, and compassion. So that's what we focus on here. We don't even talk about drugs. All we do is help students learn to live a life around two habits: *200 Percent Accountability* and *Each One Teach One.*"

Street and prison life foster an attitude where you cover up for others' crimes and never "rat" on anyone. At the Academy, 200 percent accountability means that everyone is accountable not only for their own behavior (the first 100 percent) but for the behavior of everyone else in the house (the second 100 percent). The ethic is so rigorously practiced that in recent years police departments have sent their officers to learn peer accountability from these former criminals.[3]

"Each One Teach One" means that rather than living the self-centered life of the past, you become responsible for the growth and success of your peers. Once you learn something, you're responsible to teach it to your brothers and sisters. The entire Academy is run by peers. There are no "professional" outside staff members. Every aspect of the businesses they run, including an award-winning boutique, storage business, construction company, and moving company are run by older peers who mentor younger peers in learning marketing, sales, operations, logistics, and so on.

While the commercial success of the Academy businesses is impressive, revenue is not their mission. The mission is deep and lasting change. And evidence suggests that these habits contribute significantly to that result. Before attending the Academy, students had a veritable 100 percent record of rearrest. By contrast, 92 percent of three-year graduates of The Other Side Academy remain drug free, crime free, and employed over the next three to five years.

A key to the success of The Other Side Academy, and all effective influence efforts, is clarity about the vital behaviors they want to foster. Even with very complex problems, the second key to influence is to identify one or two vital behaviors that will have the greatest impact on the results you're after.

So how do you find these disproportionately effective habits if they're not glaringly evident? The most efficient way is by studying something called "positive deviance."

## Act Like an Influencer

A bank executive bragged that she had identified the vital behavior for winning a Dragon Boat race. Her bank sponsored a team that raced outriggers across Tampa Bay. The vital behavior she had in mind? Drumroll please: it's *paddling*. The executive laughed, but she was also serious: "In the middle of a race, people start to argue about strategies and tactics, and then somebody yells, 'Shut up and paddle!' That's when you win the race!" Often it's the obvious but underused habits that prove vital.

## Find Vital Behaviors by Studying Positive Deviance

Sometimes the behavior you want to influence is obvious. You want colleagues to show up better prepared for meetings, you hope patients will take their medications properly after discharge from the hospital, or you'd like theme park customers to throw their refuse in trash receptacles. The behavior you need is obvious. But as we just saw at The Other Side Academy, sometimes you know the *results* you're after but aren't sure what *behaviors* will make the biggest difference. In those cases, look for positive deviance.

Positive deviance occurs when an individual or group *should* have the problem you're trying to solve but doesn't. In other words, they deviate from the norm in a positive direction.

For example, the Covid-19 pandemic was tough on all industries, *especially healthcare*. Like most hospital systems across the United States, HCA Healthcare experienced high nursing turnover. Some hospitals were losing 40 to 50 percent of their most skilled nurses annually. Eye-popping contract labor offers, often twice what the nurses were currently earning, led to bidding wars that were unsustainable across the industry. Jennifer Berres, HCA Healthcare's CHRO, suspected their problem was not just economics. She suspected that there were opportunities to improve the situation by influencing how leaders shaped and impacted the employee experience.

Berres asked two of her leaders, Lisa Doyle and Laura Grams, to start by looking for positive deviance. They searched for hospitals within their system, or units within hospitals, that were subject to the same market conditions and competition for talent as others but were retaining nurses at a higher rate. And they found some. They found hospitals and units that had 60 to 70 percent lower turnover than their peers even though they were of similar size and operated in equally competitive labor markets.

Next, they looked at what those hospitals were doing differently and uncovered vital behaviors—patterns of leadership behavior that were starkly different in positive deviant hospitals compared to struggling peers. Here's what they found.

The vital behaviors: leaders create regular experiences that help nurses know:

1. Leadership *cares* about them.
2. *Help* is available when they need it.
3. They have opportunities for professional *growth.*

As they focused their influence efforts on these behaviors, they saw significant and rapid reductions in turnover in 26 out of 28 of their highest priority facilities.

Dr. Donald Hopkins used the same method to find one vital behavior for eradicating the dreaded Guinea worm. While most villages they studied were rife with infections year after year, they would occasionally find one that sometimes drew water from the same infected ponds as a neighbor, but where Guinea worm infections rarely occurred. Dr. Hopkins and his colleagues followed villagers to the pond and soon understood why. Villagers from high infection areas would bring a single gourd or bucket to the pond, fill it with compromised water, then return to the village to use it.

Their positive deviant neighbors by contrast brought *two* gourds to the pond. They immersed one in the pond, then covered the second with a piece of cloth and poured the water into it. The first vital behavior was discovered!

Effective leaders understand that influence is about changing behavior. They set themselves up for success by clearly identifying the one or two actions that, if practiced consistently, will create a cascade of change.

> *See how one school system found the vital behaviors*
> *to overcome leadership turnover.*
> *Read the KIPP case study at CrucialInfluence.com.*

## KEY 3: ENGAGE ALL SIX SOURCES OF INFLUENCE

The third and final key to influence lies in finding a way to get people to adopt new vital behaviors. You've identified what you want. You know what behaviors it will take to get you there. Now you have to get people to actually do them. But how?

As we said earlier, everyone has a theory of influence. Every idea you come up with for influencing others is shaped by that theory. The problem is that most of our theories revolve around one source of influence. Usually, we resort to some sort of incentive or punishment. In reality, though, there are a variety of sources of influence that affect people's motivation as well as their ability to adopt the vital behaviors.

We've created a model of the six different sources, or categories, of influence that determine human behavior. If you want to amplify your influence, you need to learn to think categorically. Every time you think of a way of influencing others, ask yourself, "Which source of influence does this idea employ?" This practice is a helpful nudge to ensure you explore all possible sources of influence.

The reason this discipline is so vital is that effective leaders over-determine success. In other words, great leaders put all six sources of influence to work to make change inevitable.

> *Effective leaders succeed where the rest of us fail because they overdetermine success.*

Less effective leaders do the opposite: they *under*determine change. They come up with one idea—focusing on one source of influence—and put it into practice. When they fail to see substantive change, they either give up or try another source of influence. That's the equivalent of asking six strong people to help you push a stalled vehicle, one at a time.

If it's true that six sources of influence shape our choices, and all you change is one of them, that means the other five are still support-ing the old norms. Our research shows that leaders who learn the dis-cipline of recognizing and engaging all six sources of influence are not just *incrementally* more effective, they are *exponentially* so. The odds of you seeing rapid, profound, and sustainable behavior change go up 1,000 percent when you overdetermine change.[4]

Let's take a quick look at these six sources. We'll then spend the rest of the book examining them in detail and learning how to apply them to solve your own influence challenges.

## Source 1. Personal Motivation

We'll start with the source people most frequently include in their lead-ership attempts: personal motivation. As you watch others not doing the right thing while repeatedly doing the wrong thing, ask: *Do they get pleasure or a sense of meaning from doing the wrong thing?* In most cases—particularly with deep-rooted behavior—this source of influence is an important factor in propelling and sustaining change.

Let's return to Dr. Donald Hopkins and the race to eradicate Guinea worm disease. Once his team determined a vital behavior that would prevent the spread (filtering water before consuming it), they needed to influence people to actually do the behavior required. They used all six sources of influence to achieve that.

For example, Dr. Hopkins knows villagers won't filter their water unless they *feel* a sense of purpose for doing so (e.g., *I want to protect my children from miserable infections!*). So, as we'll see later, Dr. Hopkins develops influence methods to frame water filtering as a way of protecting children for those he tries to influence.

## Source 2. Personal Ability

Of course, motivation isn't everything. When trying to understand why others don't do what they should do, ask: *Can they do it?* Just because individuals enjoy doing something doesn't mean they'll succeed. They need to have the skills, talent, and understanding required to enact each vital behavior or they'll fail.

For example, it's easier to get water filtering wrong than right. If you use a loosely woven cloth, or if you filter one gourd on one side of the cloth, then turn it the other way on the next gourd, or if you fail to completely cover the opening of your vessel, larvae may sneak through. Skill matters. Engaging villagers in hands-on practice supervised by competent peers made a big difference in eradicating Guinea worm.

## Source 3. Social Motivation

Next, you need to examine the social side of influence by asking: *Do others encourage them to enact the wrong behavior?*

Despite the tremendous potential benefit of filtering water in villages, few pick up the new habit until those they respect do it first. No one wants to look like a misfit. Dr. Hopkins was careful to consider not just the message but the messengers he used to encourage the new behaviors. He chose formal leaders and influential community members to help carry his message.

## Source 4. Social Ability

Others not only provide a source of motivation, but they can also enable vital behaviors. To examine this important source of influence, ask: *Do others assist them? Are they enabled to do it?* Villagers were much more likely to pick up the filtering habit when Dr. Hopkins arranged for friends to model it, provide feedback, and even loan a spare filtering cloth when needed.

## Source 5. Structural Motivation

Even leaders who think about both individual and social factors are often blind to the role "things" play in encouraging and enabling vital behaviors. To check for this source, ask: *Are they rewarded for doing it, or punished for not doing it?*

Dr. Hopkins often used token rewards for doing the new behavior to jumpstart change—a T-shirt here and a bag of rice there can help people attempt an uncomfortable new habit.

## Source 6. Structural Ability

Finally, the physical and virtual environments we're in, and the structure of our work and social systems, can either encourage or discourage performance. To examine this source, ask: *Does their environment enable them?*

For example, Dr. Hopkins and his team encouraged village leaders to fence off access to ponds except at certain access points. That made it easier to have experts observe water-gathering to ensure everyone was practicing good filtering habits.

So, there they are—the three keys to influence. Whether you're eradicating disease or improving customer service, these three principles provide the foundation of all effective influence strategies. They aren't tricks or gimmicks. They aren't fads or the "latest things." They aren't quick fixes. But together they make up a *learnable* path to success. They are the science of leading change.

# PART II

## THE SIX SOURCES
## OF INFLUENCE

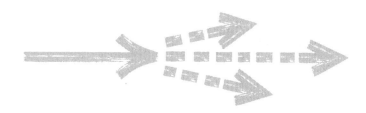

Most of us have an influence bias—and don't even realize it. We have a favorite source of influence we reflexively lean on when trying to help others change. One of the fastest ways to amplify your influence is to learn to spot your bias, then broaden your options.

For example, imagine you're a healthcare CEO. You have a fancy new artificial intelligence system to help doctors better diagnose and treat patients. The problem is since you announced the mandatory use of the new system, a grand total of 12 percent of your doctors have begun using it. Some have become openly hostile. You've been accused of everything from "replacing medicine with a cookbook" to "dehumanizing healthcare." What will you do?

Now be careful. The way you answer that question gives a hint about your influence bias. Will you invoke consequences? Make a moral argument? Invest in more training? Or perhaps offer incentives? Each of these options represents a different category of influence. Most of us have favorite categories. And the problem with favorites is that they undermine our influence. They tempt us to demand that people respond to the single source of influence we wield rather than the many that shape them.

But people bet on single-source influence strategies all the time. Ask leaders how they're planning to change their employees from being clock-punchers to customer zealots, and they'll point to their new training program—the same one that made Disney a master of the customer experience. The training content might provide a start, but when it comes to creating a culture of service, it'll take a great deal more than a course. Ask politicians what they're doing to reduce homelessness, and they'll tell you that they're building thousands of deeply affordable tiny homes. Their hope is that housing availability (a single source of influence) will solve homelessness. But housing alone is unlikely to have much of an impact if many other sources of influence are at play with the unsheltered people they're trying to help.

All of us have yearned for a quick fix for a complex problem. A powerful phrase for holding people accountable, a magical marriage solution, a two-hour course that will change your work culture from a short- to a long-term orientation.

But as H. L. Mencken said, "there is always a well-known solution to every human problem—neat, plausible, and wrong."[1]

If the behavior you're trying to change is supported only by one source of influence, changing that one might be sufficient to improve results. However, when you're facing long-standing, highly established habits, you're typically up against many—if not all six—sources of influence. If six sources are driving a bad habit and you address only one, what do you predict will happen?

If you answered, "Nothing," you're right. The problem is not a mystery. It's math.

For the rest of this book, we're going to learn about the Six Sources of Influence in depth. To understand how the sources are related, you need to first know why we've organized them the way we have.

## MOTIVATION AND ABILITY

Virtually all forces that influence human behavior work on one of two drivers. At the end of the day a person asks, "Can I do it?" and, "Will it be worth it?"

The first question simply asks, "Am I able?" The second, "Am I motivated?" *Motivation* and *ability* make up the two columns of our six-source model. Our research shows most leaders tend to live on the left side of the model and rarely look at the right. They tend to overestimate the amount of motivation required to influence change, and grossly underestimate the degree to which *ability* plays a role.

For example, a friend asks you for advice to change his eating habits. "My doctor tells me to try to eat about 2,000 calories a day," he laments. "Yesterday I ate 5,286 calories. I finished the day by downing an entire tub of Ben and Jerry's ice cream in my hotel room. Why do I keep doing this?"

How would you answer your friend's question? Why is he continually overshooting his caloric intention by such a colossal amount?

Typical answers include, "Ben and Jerry's is yummy," or, "You were stressed," or, "You lack self-control," or a fan favorite: "You eat your feelings."

Whatever your answer, ask yourself, did you assume it was a motivation problem or an ability problem?

If you're like most people, you defaulted to motivation.

How you answer the "Why are they doing this?" question will drive how you attempt to influence change. If your answer is a simple "try harder," your theory of influence probably looks like the following figure.

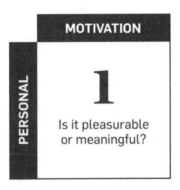

Personal Motivation

We've put the question of "why do people do what they do?" to tens of thousands of leaders across the world. Less than 1 percent of the time does someone respond with, "Perhaps they lack some skills."

One of the most powerful uses of the Six Sources of Influence is to develop the habit of examining the world through each of the sources as you diagnose the behavior you'd like to change.

Every time you consider the causes of someone's behavior, look at both sides of the model and ask, "How does motivation play a role?" then "How about ability?" This discipline will increase your influence exponentially.

## PERSONAL, SOCIAL, AND STRUCTURAL INFLUENCES

Behavior is driven by motivation and ability, and those drivers can both be broken down into three helpful subcategories: personal, social, and structural.

| MOTIVATION | ABILITY |
|---|---|
| **PERSONAL** | |
| **1**<br>Is it pleasurable or meaningful? | **2**<br>Can they do it? |
| **SOCIAL** | |
| **3**<br>Are they encouraged to do it? | **4**<br>Are they enabled to do it? |
| **STRUCTURAL** | |
| **5**<br>Are they rewarded for doing it, or punished for not doing it? | **6**<br>Does their environment (both physical and virtual) enable it? |

Six Sources of Influence with Diagnostic Questions

The top row, "Personal" looks *inside* the person to understand what motivates and enables them to act the way they do. The second row, "Social," looks at all the people around them to examine how others influence their motivation and ability. And finally, the third row, "Structural," looks at how nonhuman influences (like economics, physical space, policies, and processes) motivate and enable behavior.

Let's look at an example about what happens when you consider each source as you diagnose the root of behavior you'd like to change.

One of the authors got a call one night at 9:30 p.m. He wasn't surprised to get a call. But he was surprised that it was the police. The officer said sternly, "We have your 13-year-old son, Brian, here at the station. He and his friends were throwing water balloons at cars."

As Dad drove through the dark, he fumed about his miscreant son. His *theory of influence* was simple: Brian did this because he is an impulsive teenager who has no respect for others. It was purely a problem of bad motives, and Dad had just the solution: ask the police to incarcerate him until he was 18.

Fortunately, it was a somewhat lengthy drive to the police station. As Dad had time to breathe, he began to examine the problem more carefully. Look how much richer his diagnosis was when he considered each source of influence:

| | MOTIVATION | ABILITY |
|---|---|---|
| **PERSONAL** | There are few things more satisfying to a 13-year-old than masterfully hitting a moving object.<br><br>He's 13: The feelings of the woman driving the car don't exist to him. | Seven years of little-league baseball have prepared him for this moment.<br><br>He is not skilled at thinking about complex consequences. |
| **SOCIAL** | He had four accomplices who egged each other on.<br><br>He thought that hitting a moving car would earn him status. | Others helped him fill the balloons and find a concealed spot. |
| **STRUCTURAL** | Balloons are cheap.<br><br>In the moment, there appeared to be no downside to taking the risk. | It was dark. He had the tools he needed. He was at a home where supervision is rare. |

Six Sources of Influence Applied to Throwing Water Balloons

By the time Dad pulled into the precinct, he was in a different emotional place. As he walked through the station door, he could not only see how *understandable* the bad decision was, but also had more inspired ideas about how to influence change. More on what he did later.

How you explain someone's behavior determines how you feel about their behavior. When your diagnosis is more complete, your feelings become more nuanced.

Our goal in the coming chapters is to persuade you of three things:

1. **The power of the Six Sources of Influence.** As you come to appreciate the potency of each source of influence, you'll become convinced of the dangers of neglecting any of them.

2. **The possibilities for engaging every source.** As we describe how leaders across the world use each source of influence, we hope you see how dynamic they are.

3. **The hope for real change when you engage all six sources.** The cumulative message is that it is possible to think in more intentional ways about the most important work we ever do: influencing human behavior.

> *Do you currently face a change challenge?* Take our Crucial Influence assessment to see how well you apply multiple sources of influence—and how you can improve. Take the assessment at www.CrucialInfluence.com.

## À LA CARTE IS OK TOO

Don't feel guilty if you get a single great idea from a chapter and decide to use it without addressing all six sources of influence. Much of the time you're just trying to persuade someone to attend a meeting, and you don't need to pull out the six-source model and conduct a full diagnosis.

For these simpler influence challenges, feel free to use ideas "à la carte" and see how they work. You don't always have to use all six sources of influence to create change. However, when simpler efforts fail, use the full model to diagnose the reason and to figure out how to supplement your effort to achieve greater success.

|  | MOTIVATION | ABILITY |
| --- | --- | --- |
| **PERSONAL** | **Help Them Love What They Hate** | Help Them Do What They Can't |
| **SOCIAL** | Provide Encouragement | Provide Assistance |
| **STRUCTURAL** | Change Their Economy | Change Their Environment |

# 3

# HELP THEM LOVE
# WHAT THEY HATE

## *Source 1: Personal Motivation*

---

*It's possible to change how people feel about almost any behavior. Good leaders help people love what they might otherwise hate, using four powerful reframing tactics.*

---

We'll start our exploration of the Six Sources of Influence by examining tactics that address source 1, *personal motivation*. This important source of influence answers the question: Is the vital behavior intrinsically pleasurable or meaningful? Or is it painful?

The first problem leaders face is that good behaviors often feel bad while bad behaviors feel good. For example, to eradicate the dreaded Guinea worm disease we mentioned earlier, leaders have to get 3 million people who are suffering the terrible agony associated with an emerging worm to avoid doing the one thing that would bring them immediate relief—soaking their infected limbs in the water. How could you possibly hope to convince others to do something so painful and difficult?

But it's not just Guinea worm disease eradication that demands that people find a way to do what they don't like doing. Think about it. The vast majority of the intractable influence problems we face or the stretch goals we routinely miss are made more daunting because bad things are fun and good things aren't.

For example, tens of thousands of people die in hospitals each year because healthcare workers don't always wash their hands properly. Why? In part because it's tedious. But it can also even be painful to do it for the eighty-seventh time in a day. Likewise, Danny Meyer, the New York restaurateur, has to find a way to help thousands of employees take pleasure in going to extraordinary lengths to serve clients who are sometimes unruly or even petulant.

Can you help others *want* to do something that they currently *don't want* to do? Is it possible to help others learn to love what they presently hate?

## TUESDAY AFTERNOON AT THE OTHER SIDE ACADEMY

It's 3:17 on a Tuesday afternoon. Jessica is carrying food plates to a couple of fellow students who are not feeling well.* Usually, Jessica is responsible for finances, but the culinary services crew boss was short-staffed and asked her to help out. So she arranged coverage of her desk, and here she was carefully carrying plates to the ailing students' dorm.

---

* In order to protect privacy, Jessica and some other students' stories are composite cases—they draw on actual events and backstories from multiple students of both The Other Side Academy and Delancey Street Foundation.

What surprises Jessica is how quickly her feet are moving. She can't recall the last time they moved this fast. From the time she was nine, she had perfected a purposefully casual gait. She took great pride in her "I'm OK/you suck" approach to life. No matter that this attitude had landed her in jail for most of her adolescent years. No matter that it had earned her a manslaughter conviction after someone looked at her sideways in a bar. Nobody was going to tell her what to do. Nobody.

So why is Jessica walking so fast now? It's been 19 months since she was offered a place at The Other Side Academy rather than serving her third prison term. Every semester, Jessica has attended the Academy's graduation ceremony. It's a grand gathering where all the students crowd into the main hall to celebrate each other's progress. The first two times Jessica was recognized for her accomplishments, she stared at the floor and ignored whatever they were saying about her, thinking, *Who cares that I now know how to set a stupid table? This is all a pointless game, and I'm not playing it!* When the applause for Jessica had died down, she walked back to her chair, unaffected.

But at last week's graduation ceremony they had talked about her GED diploma and her promotion to crew boss. She had looked at Dave Durocher, who was remarking on how far Jessica had come, and made the mistake of listening to what he said—just for a second. Then came the wave of applause. Jessica looked around the room and caught the eyes of a few of her sisters and brothers. Then she looked quickly back down at the floor. Her legs felt weak when she walked back to her chair. "I'm not sure what that is," she mumbled to herself. "I'm probably just hungry." She ate a candy bar.

Now as Jessica rushes to the dorm, she looks down again, only this time at her legs. They're moving so fast it's as if they have a mind of their own. And then she lifts her hand to her cheek and feels something wet. *I don't do this. What the hell is this?* Jessica is crying.

## MAKE PAIN PLEASURABLE

So, what has happened to Jessica at this tender moment of an ongoing transformation? In Jessica's words, she realized in that instant that she was feeling emotions she had never felt before. She was taking pleasure in accomplishing something. She was finding joy in her work. Better still, she has learned to care about something. In Jessica's own words, "After thinking about it all afternoon, I finally realized I was crying because *I cared*. I cared that I got the food to my family. I cared *a lot*."

If Jessica has found a way to take pleasure from something that she previously disliked, what might your average person learn from this? For example, what mysterious trick might you pull in order to help your son enjoy doing his chores? Could this same magic potion help a team *enjoy* the work involved in reducing errors to below 3.4 per million? And can you use Jessica's mystical elixir to make eating mini carrots as enjoyable as wolfing down a slice of chocolate cream pie?

People learn ways to take pleasure from almost any activity, even if the activity isn't inherently satisfying.

Social psychologist Jonathan Haidt makes this point rather bluntly: "Just because a desire or behavior is natural, does not mean it is . . . unchangeable. . . . It is also natural . . . to never brush our teeth. Yet we teach ourselves to do the unnatural. Another characteristic of human nature—perhaps the one that makes us more human—is our capacity to do the unnatural, to transcend and hence transform our own nature."[1]

We're extending this argument even further. Humans don't merely find ways to act unnaturally. They find ways to enjoy activities that aren't inherently enjoyable. Depending on your point of view, hand-washing in a hospital can feel like either a tedious distraction or a sacred duty. Finishing tasks on time can feel like either a bureaucratic bore or a demonstration of integrity. Changing a baby's diaper can feel like either a gruesome chore or a precious moment. The question is, how can you help vital behaviors feel like the latter rather than the former?

## Change the Frame and You Change the Feeling

The good news is it's possible to change how people feel about almost any behavior. For example, chocolate is not inescapably tempting, and doing push-ups is not unavoidably miserable. Believe it or not, some people deeply enjoy playing repetitive games with grandchildren, running until their legs give out, mowing the lawn, or proofreading technical manuals. Why? It isn't because the nature of the activity is different for them. It's because they experience the activity differently than others. They feel different because they frame the behavior differently.

Your moral frame for an activity is your answer to the question, "What does this mean?"

For example, come with us to a popular burger joint in a busy part of town. Imagine you are the manager of this busy burger joint. You have an employee named Lou who just isn't into the whole customer-serving thing. You've been reminding him, coaching him, and even pleading with him to greet customers, thoroughly clean tables, and in other ways improve the guest experience.

Today you look over the patio eating area where you see five filthy tables, and then your eyes land on Lou, who is sitting at a table, stuffing his face with french fries, and sending a text message. What will you do? Think about it. If you had to craft one sentence to influence Lou, what would it be?

Now, examine your sentence. What method of influence did you employ? If you're like most of us, your sentence was some form of nag, guilt, or threat. Generally, when we face a problem like Lou, we make an automatic assumption that he's simply not motivated because he takes no pleasure in doing the work. Then, without even realizing it, we make a second mental leap. We assume that the reason he's not motivated is because of some moral defect.

That may sound harsh, but think about it for a moment. When a doctor fails to wash her hands, we might assume, "She cares more about her own convenience than about patient safety!" Similarly, when Lou fails to exert himself for customers, we conclude, "He's just lazy."

This tendency to attribute others' worst behavior to some underlying character flaw is so common that psychologists have given it a special name: the *fundamental attribution error*.

## Avoid the Fundamental Attribution Error

The fundamental attribution error is the belief that people do what they do merely because they enjoy it: "Why did that bozo just cut me off in traffic? Because he's selfish and thinks the road belongs to him." Whenever others cause us inconvenience or pain, we have a natural tendency to suspect that they have selfish and malicious intentions.

The best leaders *don't* assume that others take the low road because of a moral defect. They consider that the behavior might be caused by a lack of understanding or a lack of awareness of consequences. The problem is not that these people are incapable of caring about others. It's that they aren't *thinking* about others at that particular moment.

In other words, doctors who fail to wash their hands between patients may not be uncaring. It could be that in the moment they're not thinking about germs and infections. They're thinking about examining the next patient or perhaps even comforting a patient's family member.

So if the problem with Lou is not a moral defect, but moral slumber, what can you do to wake him up? How can you infuse a crucial moment—one in which he can act in a way to better serve customers (rather than just doing grunt work)—with moral significance? Stay tuned. We'll return to Lou (and misbehaving teenager Brian) later to see how this crucial moment can be turned into a moment of influence.

## HELP OTHERS REFRAME THE BEHAVIOR

Good leaders understand how easy and important it is to influence the way people frame vital behaviors. They help people love what they might otherwise hate using four powerful reframing tactics:

1. Allow for choice.
2. Create direct experiences.
3. Tell meaningful stories.
4. Make it a game.

### Tactic 1. Allow for Choice

*Allow for choice* is at the top of our list of strategies because it's the gateway to all other methods of influencing personal motivation. As organizational scholar Peter Block put it, "If we cannot say no, then saying yes has no meaning."

You can never hope to get people's commitment if they don't have permission to say no. So long as people frame the vital behavior as a "have to" rather than a "want to," they will feel resistant rather than committed.

When others appear to be willfully misbehaving, our natural reaction is to nag, guilt, or threaten them.

"Lou! Get back to work!"

We've all done it. Perhaps you have a grown child who comes to family events late. Every single time. And when she walks in the door late, you say, "It's about time you got here!" Every single time.

We want to influence others, but we tend to do it in a way that provokes resistance rather than inviting willingness.

Top leaders approach resistance with an influence mindset. Their first goal is to ensure that the vital behavior is framed in a personally motivating way.

There is no better evidence of the efficacy of this approach than the work of University of New Mexico psychologist Dr. William Miller.

## Use the Influence of Questions

Miller has spent his long career studying how to influence addicts—those caught in self-destructive habits that offer some form of immediate gratification. Addiction is the ultimate example of bad stuff feeling good and good stuff feeling bad.

What can you possibly do to influence someone whose world seems arranged in that way? Most people with addictions have been lectured, threatened, and guilt-tripped by well-intended friends and family for years. They've often been written off by those who think they've tried everything, and conclude that their addicted friend simply doesn't want to change. So what has Miller learned about motivating those who appear unmotivated to change?

He learned that *we often mistake ambivalence for apathy*. Most addicts sincerely possess both motivations to quit and motivations to use. And most of the change tactics we try (nagging, lecturing, etc.) keep them focused on their reasons to use.

Dr. Miller's influence prescription to change the cycle is what he calls a *motivational interview.*

William Miller discovered how leaders can be
more effective at helping people choose to change.

On the way to his discovery, Dr. Miller studied the consequences of the made-for-TV "intervention" approach. The reigning theory at the time was that a well-staged confrontation between unified loved ones and the addict would compel them to confront their demons. It didn't. In fact, in one study, he found that confrontation actually *increased* alcoholic binging.

Demanding that people change rarely leads to change. So Miller began to explore alternate approaches. Decades later, his findings have become the gold standard for influencing those struggling with drug addictions, alcohol abuse, eating disorders, gambling, high-risk sex, and dozens of other overpowering habits.

A motivational interview replaces judgment with empathy, and lectures with questions. The goal is to help people connect and commit to motivations already at play to kick their habit.

This tactic is often used at The Other Side Academy. For example, Raoul, who has been at the Academy for three days, tells his tribe leader, Diego, that he is leaving. "I can't do this," Raoul says. "I just want to go get high." Diego's natural impulse might be to issue a threat: "The minute you walk out I'm calling Adult Probation and Parole and you'll do your 10-year prison term." He could also try shame: "So you want to be the same loser you were when you walked in?"

Both of these approaches assume Raoul is apathetic. But Diego knows better. He knows there is motivation to change inside of Raoul—Diego's job is to simply help him find it.

**Diego:** *"I know you want to get high. I've been there, bro. Is that all you want?"*

**Raoul:** *"No, man. I thought I could do this. I just can't."*

**Diego:** *"Yeah, the first days are pretty tough. So it sounds like you wish you could do this. Yeah?"*

**Raoul:** *"Of course. That's why I walked in. But I'm not ready."*

**Diego:** *"Why did you come here? Remind me."*

**Raoul:** *"Because I don't want my kids to have a loser dad like I did."*

**Diego:** *"How bad did you want that when you walked in? Scale of 1 to 10?"*

**Raoul:** *"A 10, man. A total 10."*

At this point, Raoul hangs his head and begins to cry. This man is not apathetic. He's ambivalent. He has a mixture of reasons to change and reasons to quit. By replacing a lecture with an interview, Diego has started to help him reconnect with motivations he already has. He has started Raoul on a path to choosing to stay.

In a motivational interview, a friend or counselor helps others reach their own conclusions about the values that are most important to them and the changes living those values might require. When you ask thought-provoking questions and then listen while others talk, they discover on their own what they must do. Then, propelled by their own aspirations and beliefs, they *choose* to make the necessary changes.

Smart leaders do the same. When facing potential resistance, they explore and connect with motivations people already have that can help them choose to change.

Let's look at a business example of motivational interviewing in action.

Ralph Heath, now president of Lockheed Martin Aeronautics, was once tasked by the company to move the fifth-generation F-22 fighter jet from drawing board to production floor in 18 months. To do so, he had to engage 4,500 engineers and technicians and change their view of what it took to invent things. Heath had to convince them that results mattered more than ideas (a tough sell with engineers) and that engineering needed to bow to production (an even tougher sell).

So Heath didn't sell; he listened. He spent weeks interviewing employees at all levels. He tried to understand their needs, frustrations, and aspirations. When he finally began sharing directives, he framed them in ways that honored the needs, concerns, and goals of those he had interviewed.

His influence didn't result from merely confronting problems but from listening to people and then framing needed behavior change in *their terms*. The now legendary turnaround of the F-22 began when Heath helped people discover what they really wanted and how it related to corporate objectives—rather than simply issuing orders.

## Change the Frame

A change of heart can't be imposed; it can only be chosen. People are capable of making enormous sacrifices when they have the choice to act on their own. An influential leader's job is to help them find their own reason to choose the vital behavior.

Ginger Graham, the CEO of the medical devices company Guidant, learned this in a crisis. After the company introduced a new cardiovascular stent, sales went through the roof. Almost overnight, good news turned into bad news as demand for the stent far outstretched supply. And all this hit as the holidays were approaching.

Meeting demand until new sources of production could come online would require three-shift workdays and seven-day workweeks. Graham could have simply mandated the work and required people to fulfill their obligations, but she knew that wouldn't work. It would be unfair to force this family-unfriendly schedule on employees when they deserved time off. And doing so would likely provoke resentment and hurt productivity.

So instead, Graham asked for help. At an all-company meeting, she praised the work that had brought about the wonderful achievement. She read success stories from doctors who were using the stent to avoid bypass surgery and save patients' lives. She shared sales data that showed how many unmet needs would result if supply couldn't be stepped up substantially. And then she made a request. "We have the chance to do something [for patients and for ourselves] that no company has ever done in the history of our industry. We have an obligation to rise to the challenge. And if you'll rise to the challenge, we'll do all we can to make your lives easier during the tough times." She offered a new frame and was rewarded with a new level of personal motivation.

Within half an hour, employees had made a list of all the things management could do to help them through the holidays—including shopping for their presents, wrapping them, supplying late-night taxis, bringing in pizza, and so on.

Production hit new records, and the stent was available on time for all patients who needed it.

Total sales almost tripled in one quarter. Employees earned nice bonuses. But more importantly, the employees who went through this experience felt as if they were part of something important. A moral quest.

When you swap coercive methods with personal choices, you open up the possibility of influencing even the most addictive and entrenched behaviors. You gain access to one of the most powerful human motivations: the power of the committed heart.

People can actually love engaging in behaviors that otherwise might seem obnoxious. But only if they're allowed the psychological freedom to choose them.

## Tactic 2. Create Direct Experiences

The most powerful way to help people recognize, feel, and believe in the long-term implications of their choices is to get out of their way and let them experience them firsthand.

For example, healthcare safety expert Dr. Don Berwick once taught a Harvard seminar for CEOs of some of the largest hospital systems in the world. The list of attendees was a literal Who's Who of patient safety. These leaders were sipping lattes, jotting notes, and having a delightful seminar experience as they learned ways to improve the overall health-care experience and eliminate costly hospital errors. And although it was a stimulating *intellectual* experience, Dr. Berwick had seen this happen so many times before that he knew the stimulating-lecture format would influence *no one*. All would return home, say they had a great time, email their notes to their management team, and generate no real change.

Dr. Don Berwick overcame resistance by inviting executives into a direct experience of a medical mistake.

"Then I had an idea," Dr. Berwick told us. "On the spur of the moment, I said, 'Look, before you come to the session next month, find an injured patient, someone who was harmed while in your hospital. And *you* investigate the injury. Do not delegate it. You find out what happened and come back and report it.'"

Dr. Berwick was unsure what would happen. Would the CEOs complete the assignment? Would they return with diagrams or data dumps? Or would it awaken passion?

The answer was emphatic: "Unbelievable!" he said. "I didn't know this would happen, but these people came back—I'm talking three-piece suit, high-end executives—and one by one they choked up and cried as they told their stories. They described the illusions they had about their systems and how fallible they now realized they were."

As a result of this poignant firsthand experience, many of these leaders not only became champions for patient safety, but they remained champions *for the rest of their careers.*

What happened here? Dr. Berwick operated on the belief that the problem with these leaders was not some moral deficiency. These were mothers and fathers, brothers and sisters—all of whom were capable of caring about human pain and suffering. However, the healthcare world around them shielded them from the human pain and suffering caused by the current behavior of their employees. Pain, suffering, and deprivation had been turned into numbers, statistics, and charts. Patient safety for them was a "compliance" issue, not a moral imperative.

Dr. Berwick trusted that if he gave senior leaders an experience that connected them with the human consequences of their hospital's current behavior, they would truly *care.* And it did.

The most potent tactic for engaging personal motivation is *direct experience.* Everywhere we've traveled we've seen leaders develop clever ways of helping connect people with the consequences of their choices so they begin to feel differently about new and better behaviors.

### Act Like an Influencer

When Dan Schulman kicked off American Express's effort to offer more financial services to less affluent customers, he began by immersing his executive team in a direct experience of "the life of the unbanked." The team spent the day trying to tackle typical normal financial transactions using only methods available to those without bank accounts or credit cards. The experience of standing in line at check-cashing stores in dangerous areas, seeking out retail outlets to pay a utility bill with cash, wiring money, and so on created immediate empathy and a sense of moral duty to serve the new customer segment. His new team returned with both greater motivation and ability to launch a successful new product line for underserved customers.

## Ask People to "Just Try It"

People tend to resist new behaviors because they're crystal clear about what they'll lose by changing but uncertain about what they'll gain. When it comes to change, humans tend to overvalue what they're losing while undervaluing what they gain. And no amount of cheerleading will allay the fears as fast a hands-on experience.

The Other Side Academy's Dave Durocher confronts this fear of change every single day. It's his job to ask new students to do things that, to them, sound painful, boring, or both.

For example, lifetime criminals have no idea what a law-abiding life might be like. They assume that it will be very much like their present life—minus the fun. You know, cleaning toilets while giving up the excitement of crime or the stimulation of drugs. They're unable to imagine the pleasure associated with getting a raise, owning a home, or gaining any of a thousand other perks of a law-abiding life.

Durocher could spend a lot of time lecturing about the Academy vision. "Trust me," he could say, "you're gonna love it. By the time you're out of here, you'll have a high school diploma. You'll be literate. You'll have gone to concerts and museums. You'll have mastered three different trades and tried a dozen others. You'll have a whole new set of friends. Just sign here."

Right.

These arguments are hard to sell because Durocher would be describing activities and outcomes for which his audience has no frame of reference. He's also asking them to make immediate sacrifices (no gang, no drugs, no freedom) in order to achieve them.

It won't work. It can't work.

Durocher realizes that it'll take a while before new students *personally experience* the benefits of a new life. "Every one of our students leaves with at least a high school equivalency. But early on, they hate the discipline that it takes to study. Coming in, students hate everything they haven't done before. But of course they've never done *anything!*"

So Durocher simply plods forward, demanding that students try studying for a class, attending the opera, mentoring another student, and so forth. Experience has taught him that if students try new behaviors, they end up liking many, if not most of them.

Durocher sticks with the strategy of asking students to simply try things until every single one has an experience like Jessica's, when she suddenly realized she now feels wonderful about something she once didn't understand or care about.

Dave says it happens to virtually everyone at The Other Side Academy. They transform into the kind of people they've scarcely met before. They care. They take satisfaction in accomplishment. And Durocher helps them get there by inviting them to have bite-sized direct experiences.

## Act Like an Influencer

Holding a job can't be fun, right? That's why they call it work. Many young people don't expect to like work, but then they quickly change their minds once they experience it.

One of the authors has had several high-school-age nieces and nephews spend summers with him and their auntie in Park City, Utah. Park City is fun in the summer, with lots of hiking and cycling, but there's a catch. In order to play in the mountains, these young people also have to work at a job for 40 hours a week—and it's a volunteer job, where they serve wounded vets and disabled children. A typical job involves belaying at one end of a climbing rope, while the disabled vet on the other end struggles up a climbing wall.

Most of these high schoolers rebel at the very thought of volunteering for such work. However, by the end of the first week, they can't wait to show up for their shift. They see the positive impacts they are having, and they love the feelings of fulfillment.

## Tactic 3. Tell Meaningful Stories

The challenge with offering people direct experiences is that it's tough to create them for all of the people you need to influence. Is there something you can do that offers some of the power of direct experience without consuming so much time and so many resources?

### Snakes on a Campus: The Power of Vicarious Experience

To answer this important question, we'll visit the chief theorist behind many of the influence principles we're about to discover: Dr. Albert Bandura. One of Bandura's many contributions to the science of influence was his remarkable work in the 1970s with people who had phobias. His insights shined light on dealing with unmotivated—even terrified—subjects.

When Bandura came on the phobia scene, the common treatment consisted of years on a couch. The accepted theory at the time was that phobias originated in some critical childhood experience, and the only way out of them was by resurrecting and resolving those memories. Dr. Bandura took a different view. Rather than dredge up the past, he took a more direct route by creating firsthand experiences in the present.

Dr. Albert Bandura showed how vicarious and direct experiences—exposure to the very things they are most afraid of—could help people overcome their phobias.

Bandura ran an ad in the *Palo Alto News* asking readers who had a paralyzing fear of snakes to descend into the basement of the psychology department to get cured. Hundreds volunteered. All who responded had been seriously debilitated by their unreasonable fear of things that slither. Most had horrible nightmares; many were veritable shut-ins. They were desperate for help.

Like any good leader, Bandura began by defining the result he wanted to achieve and how he would measure it. Success, he decided, would be achieved when subjects could sit with a six-foot red-tailed boa constrictor draped across their lap. Could a goal be clearer?

When they began, none of the subjects would so much as enter the room containing a snake in a covered terrarium. Bandura's very description of the objective caused some to pass out.

Bandura resisted any effort to rush or coerce the subjects. Instead, he offered options and allowed them to choose. If people wanted to opt out, they could. If they wanted a simpler task, he would devise one. They were in control at all times.

Bandura's strategy began with a secondhand experience. He asked subjects to watch a research assistant handle a snake. He invited subjects to watch from the doorway of the room—or if that was still too difficult, to watch through glass—as the assistant walked into the room containing the snake, took a look at it, opened the terrarium, petted the snake, and finally removed the boa and placed it on his or her lap.

After the subjects watched someone else handle the snake, Dr. Bandura invited them to have a direct experience. First they would simply walk into the room. Some of the subjects asked for protective gear—hockey goalie gloves, a baseball catcher chest protector and mask, and so on.

Subjects entered the room and stood next to the enclosed tank. Gradually, after several tries, they worked up to removing the terrarium cover and then quickly retreating from the room. No harm done. After a bit more experience, they finally touched the snake. Then they touched the snake without gloves, and so forth. Eventually subjects sat in the room by themselves with the six-foot boa constrictor draped across their lap.

And now for the real miracle: the entire process took only three hours!

People who had been debilitated most of their lives by a paralyzing fear were completely cured in a single morning. And the results lasted a lifetime.

Once the subjects with snake phobias had a personal and positive interaction with the snake, they never regressed, and it improved their lives forever.

In Dr. Bandura's own words, "It was surprising to see how liberating it was for the subjects to be freed from the phobia. Their whole life seemed to open up before them now that they didn't have to worry about snakes. In addition, they gained confidence about their ability to make personal changes. Since they had been able to conquer their fear of snakes, perhaps now they could overcome other problems."

## The Influence of a Story

Another way of creating vicarious experience is through storytelling. This powerful influence tool is available to all leaders and requires zero resources and very little time.

Although it clearly takes more than a story to drive change, when used in combination with other sources of influence, storytelling is an essential tool in any leader's repertoire.

The most convincing field experiment in the entire history of behavioral science research makes exactly this point. In 1993, Martha Swai changed the behavior of an entire nation by simply telling a story.

Swai was the program manager for Radio Tanzania. Her goal was to change the behavior of her fellow Tanzanians in order to strengthen families, improve the lot of women, and save lives from HIV/AIDS. Televisions were not widely available in Tanzania, so as a program manager for a radio station, she had access to millions of ears every single night.

Swai hired the best dramatic writers she could find to create a story showing the vital behaviors she wanted to effect and the consequences of ignoring them.

Swai's task wasn't easy because those she was trying to influence held deep beliefs about how men should relate to women and about what causes AIDS and what cures it. For one, many thought that men could be cured of AIDS by having sex with a virgin.

When the time came to launch the radio show, disaster struck. Bureaucratic problems blocked Radio Tanzania transmission during the show's airtime to the large Dodoma region of central Tanzania. This programming barrier turned into a social science bonanza—as we'll shortly see.

In 1993 the show *Twende na Wakati* ("Let's Go with the Times") hit the airwaves. To demonstrate the cause and effect of AIDS, writers created a flamboyant, macho, and highly controversial truck driver named Mkwaju. He abused his wife, wanted only male children, drank excessively, engaged in unprotected sex with prostitutes along his route, and bragged about his escapades. His wife, Tutu (a model for female independence), eventually left him and succeeded in her own small business.

Over the course of many months, the philandering Mkwaju (who eventually died of AIDS) became so real to the listening audience that when the actor playing him went to a local vegetable market, women who recognized his voice threw produce at him!

To see the emotional and behavioral impact firsthand, we interviewed several listening groups just outside Tanzania's capital city. One family group consisting of a father, mother, grandmother, aunt, and five grown children had religiously tuned in to the wild antics of Mkwaju and had been enormously affected. When we asked them how the program had influenced them, the father explained that at first he had admired Mkwaju, but with time he concluded that the truck driver's behavior was causing pain to his wife, Tutu, and their children.

And one day, when sweet Tutu was hurt by her alcoholic husband, a light went on—his own wife was also suffering from similar treatment. Although this avid listener wasn't a truck-driving philanderer, he had abused alcohol. A part of him was Mkwaju.

From that moment on he stopped abusing alcohol and his family members. It seemed strange that this self-discovery would come through a contrived radio show, but as the transformed father finished his story, everyone in his family nodded in energetic agreement. He had truly changed.

Similar interviews provided anecdotal evidence that *Twende na Wakati* was more than just a story. It created a poignant, believable vicarious experience. It didn't merely provoke emotions. It changed minds. It changed people's moral arithmetic about their choices in a way that led to lasting change.

But the evidence for the efficacy of Martha Swai's work goes far beyond our anecdotal interviews. *Twende na Wakati* accidentally became the first controlled national field experiment in history. Since the Dodoma region of Tanzania was excluded from the evening radio broadcasts, researchers could explore the effect of the vicarious experiences offered over the radio.

Renowned social scientists Everett Rogers and Arvind Singhal found that one-fourth of the population in the broadcast area had modified its behavior in critical ways to avoid HIV, whereas no similar change had occurred in areas where the show wasn't available. The impact was so remarkable that the controlled experiment had to be stopped after two years in order to make the intervention available to everyone. Within a year, similar results were seen in Dodoma. People who tuned in to *Twende na Wakati* were more likely to seek marital counseling, make better use of family planning, remain faithful to their spouses, and use protection.

Storytelling isn't just for TV and radio. Time and again we watched leaders awaken people to the profound choices they were making by telling believable and compelling stories that put a human face on people's actions. Independent of the industry—whether healthcare, IT, financial services, manufacturing, or telecommunications—leaders who effectively build a sense of mission in their organizations are *always* storytellers.

Take, for example, Union Square Hospitality Group (USHG) where Danny Meyer trains leaders to use stories to turn dining hospitality into a human mission. At the Shake Shack one day, the "Lou" episode we described earlier played out in real life. As Lou malingered in the dining area of the Shake Shack, his supervisor approached him and said, "Hey Lou, a few minutes ago a young mother walked into our patio area holding the hand of her three-year-old daughter. She set her daughter up on a chair and walked to the window to order their food. While her back was turned, her daughter began sweeping her hand back and forth across the table that was smeared with ketchup from a previous guest. Then she began licking her hand."

Lou cringed. He didn't even wait for his boss to finish the *story*—but instead, rushed to grab a rag and began wiping down the tables.

What happened here? The supervisor made a connection. Rather than relying on verbal persuasion to nag or threaten, she created a vicarious experience. She told a story that helped awaken Lou to the moral content of his actions. The frame changed, and the feeling followed.

Now, is it possible that Lou may need more than this to become a hospitality zealot? Yes! The remaining chapters add just such richness. But personal motivation is a great start.

When influential leaders recognize that others aren't personally motivated to enact a vital behavior, they don't work *around* that problem. They work *through* it. They operate on the confidence that people are not morally defective, but morally asleep. When called for, they create vicarious experiences through telling compelling stories.

On that fateful night when one of the authors retrieved his delinquent son from the police station, the initial silence in the car was deafening. Finally, Dad pulled to the side of the road and said, "Hey Brian, it's been a tough day, hasn't it?" Brian looked at his father suspiciously, then conceded, "Yes, it's been awful." Dad continued, "I understand, son. I've made mistakes, too. There will be consequences to face, but you'll get through this." Brian seemed to relax. Dad continued, "But you know what, Brian? There's someone else who had a tough night, too. Can you think of who that is?"

Brian looked confused, then said, "No. Who?"

Dad said, "Imagine you're driving a car and suddenly a big hard object slams into your windshield. Maybe even cracks it. How would that feel?"

Brian looked startled by the question. Then he hung his head and said, "Dad, I don't have to guess how she felt. I know how she felt, because after she slammed on the brakes I could see her put her head down on her steering wheel. I think she was crying."

In the first moments after a critical incident, leaders have an opportunity to frame the moment. The first words out of your mouth let others know what this is about. Is it about obeying rules? Is it about protecting the family's reputation in the community? Or is it about the safety of a human being? How differently would that moment have gone if Dad had started with a lecture, punishment, or stony silence? Instead, he drew his son into a vicarious experience and offered the opportunity for him to reframe his decision to throw a water balloon.

Moments later in the car, Brian said, "Dad, do you think I could get that woman's phone number? I'd like to call her and apologize." When you change the frame, you change the feeling.

## Tactic 4. Make It a Game

Let's look at one more way of transforming neutral or detestable vital behaviors into something enjoyable.

It turns out that one of the keys to personal motivation lies in a force just barely outside the activity itself. It lies in the mastery of increasingly challenging goals. Mihaly Csikszentmihalyi, a researcher at Claremont Graduate School, has devoted his career to "flow," or the feeling of enjoyment that comes from losing yourself in an engrossing activity (something, he suggests, we all should be seeking with dogged determination).

Dr. Csikszentmihalyi discovered that almost any activity can be engaging if it involves reasonably challenging goals and clear, frequent feedback. These are the elements that turn a chore into something that feels more like a game. And we all like games.

For example, imagine that you removed the scoreboard from a basketball court. Not too many fans would stick around without knowing the score. And how long do you think the players would run breathlessly up and down the court?

Much of what we do to transform intrinsically unpleasant behavior into something enjoyable is merely turning it into a game.

Consider the elements of an enjoyable game:

- **Keeping score.** Clear, frequent feedback can transform tasks into accomplishments that, in turn, can generate intense satisfaction. The designers of many of today's video games have an intuitive feel for Dr. Csikszentmihalyi's research and have used it to create games that call for highly repetitive activities that end up being amazingly addictive as individuals strive for that next level of achievement.
- **Competition.** Seeing numbers does more than provide data. It frames the data with meaning: Am I doing better than *before*? Am I doing better than *others*? This element is more questionable (it can lead to unhealthy rivalry)—but to be honest, competition, especially with oneself, can help people take satisfaction from what would otherwise be a repetitive task.
- **Constant improvement.** How many of us track our daily step count or screen time on a smartphone or watch? The proliferation of tools to enable "the measured life" have made tracking sleep habits, blood pressure, and fitness tasks a global obsession that has helped reframe unpleasant habits into gamified satisfaction.
- **Control.** Earned points and rewards should be in the participants' control. At work people often miss this element when their personal or team progress is folded into a larger, less successful unit's overall results. Employees lose any sense of control over their own contributions. Create and record measures individuals can control. Let them see the impact of their work. For many, the impact is far more rewarding than the job itself.

By tapping into the intrinsic human desire for accomplishment, competition, improvement, and control, gamifying vital behaviors can naturally amplify personal motivation.

## SUMMARY: PERSONAL MOTIVATION

We often don't act in our long-term best interest because gratification from our short-term bad actions is real and immediate, whereas negative consequences are often fuzzy, maybe not so bad after all, and most certainly a long time off.

The good news is that how people experience behaviors can change. You can come to love things you previously hated, and you can come to hate things you previously found irresistible. Much of this transformation happens through framing—how you frame is how you feel. Influential leaders help others change how they feel by using four powerful reframing tactics:

1. Allow for choice.
2. Create direct experiences.
3. Tell meaningful stories.
4. Make it a game.

A change of heart can't be imposed; it can only be chosen. People are capable of making enormous sacrifices when they have the choice to act on their own. An influential leader's job is to help them find their own reason to choose the vital behavior.

|  | MOTIVATION | ABILITY |
|---|---|---|
| **PERSONAL** | Help Them Love What They Hate | **Help Them Do What They Can't** |
| **SOCIAL** | Provide Encouragement | Provide Assistance |
| **STRUCTURAL** | Reward with Care | Change the Environment |

# 4

# HELP THEM DO WHAT THEY CAN'T

*Source 2: Personal Ability*

---

*When you develop the discipline to examine possible ability barriers,*
*you substantially increase your potential for effective influence.*

---

Let's turn now to source 2, *personal ability*. As we move to the right side of the model, we don't just add another source of influence—we challenge our default way of understanding and influencing behavior. Our natural tendency is to attribute most negative behavior to motivation problems and almost never consider whether *ability* is playing a role. If you want to influence change, it's best to do the opposite: consider ability problems first, motivation second.

Consider the case of Henry who is currently struggling to drop the 50 pounds he's added since his job started putting him on the road where, twice a week, he now eats at delightful restaurants. Henry has joined a team of coworkers who are collectively trying to lose weight (partly to keep their insurance costs in control and partly to feel better), but he's not doing that well. One of Henry's vital behaviors—snacking on mini carrots rather than chocolate—is at risk. In fact, at this very moment, Henry is pulling the foil back on a partially eaten Swiss chocolate bar. In Henry's defense, he didn't buy it. A colleague who just returned from Europe and knew of his deep affection for chocolate gave it to him. The tempting bar has been sitting on his desk for over a week.

Moments ago Henry decided to heft the hardy confection merely to see what two pounds felt like. When he did, he noticed that the adhesive holding the wrapper around the inner foil lining had failed. It appeared as if it were about to fall away, seductively revealing the beautiful red, shiny foil beneath it—the last defense before the chocolate itself.

Henry tugged at the wrapper playfully, and with almost no effort it came free. The next few seconds were almost a blur. Without thinking, Henry's hands peeled back the top flap of the foil and exposed the deep, rich color of the bar. In a rush, chocolate-filled childhood memories poured through his head as his fingers pried loose a single section—a modest, harmlessly small packet of pleasure. He brought the treat to his lips—and then it was over. The chocolate began its inexorable transformation from cocoa, fat, and sugar to disappointment.

Here's the problem. While Henry's taste buds are delivering pleasure, his soul is racked with shame. His problem, he is convinced, is that he's weak. He's doomed to caloric servitude because he has no character, grit, or willpower. Up until this sad indulgence, he had valiantly cut back on calories while sincerely promising himself to start an exercise regimen. This new, iron-willed Henry ruled for eight full days. And then the mere touch of the red foil lining brought him to ruin.

Henry doubts he'll ever overcome the genetic hand that he's been dealt. He has neither the self-discipline to diet nor the determination to exercise. Surely he's doomed to a life of poor health. But then again, unbeknownst to Henry, a long line of research suggests that he can actually learn how to withstand the temptations of chocolate as well as how to improve his ability to exercise properly.

Many of the stories Henry has been carrying in his head since he was a young man may be equally wrong. When his mother once told him that he wasn't a gifted speaker and later when his father suggested that leadership "wasn't his thing," Henry believed that he hadn't been born with "the right stuff." He wasn't born to be an elite athlete; that's for certain. Later he learned that music wasn't his thing, and his interpersonal skills weren't all that strong. Later still he discovered that spending in excess, getting hooked on video games, and gorging on Swiss chocolate *were* his thing. But none of this is going to change, he concludes, because Henry can't fight genetics.

Fortunately, Henry is wrong. Henry is trapped in what Stanford psychologist Carol Dweck calls a "fixed mindset."[1] If he believes he can't improve, then he won't even try, and he'll create a self-fulfilling prophecy. But Henry is in luck. Genes don't play the fatalistic role scholars once assumed. Characteristics that had long been described by scholars and philosophers as genetic gifts or lifelong personality traits appear to be learned, much the same way one learns to walk, talk, or whistle.

That means Henry doesn't need to accept his current status. He can adopt what Dweck refers to as a "growth mindset." Henry simply needs to learn how to learn. But he won't take that step until he first understands that his problem is one of ability as much as motivation. This pivotal insight is a key difference between successful influence and repeated failure.

To illustrate this point, let's consider the lengthy hunt researchers conducted to find the root of self-discipline.

Dr. Dweck's research on mindset has had a significant impact on fields such as education, business, and sports.

Professor Walter Mischel of Columbia University, curious about people's inability to withstand temptations, set out to explore this issue. Did certain humans have the right stuff while others didn't? And if so, did the right stuff affect lifelong performance? What Mischel learned altered the psychological landscape forever.

## MUCH OF WILL IS SKILL

When Timmy, age four, sat down at the gray metal table in an experimental room in the basement of the psychology department, he saw something that caught his interest. On the table was a marshmallow—the kind Timmy's mom put into his hot chocolate. Timmy *really* wanted to eat the marshmallow.

The kindly man who brought Timmy into the room told him that he had two options. The man was going to step out for a moment. If Timmy wanted to eat the marshmallow, he could. But if he waited a few minutes until the man returned, then Timmy could eat *two* marshmallows.

Then the man exited. Timmy stared at the tempting sugar treat, squirmed in his chair, kicked his feet, and in general tried to exercise self-control. If he could wait, he'd get two marshmallows! But the temptation proved too strong. Timmy reached across the table, grabbed the marshmallow, looked around nervously, and shoved the spongy treat into his mouth.

Timmy was one of dozens of subjects Dr. Mischel and his colleagues studied for more than four decades.[2] Mischel was interested in learning what percentage of his youngsters could delay gratification and what impact, if any, this character trait would have on their adult lives. Mischel's hypothesis was that children who were able to demonstrate self-control at a young age would enjoy greater success later in life because of that trait.

In this and many similar studies, Mischel followed the children into adulthood. He discovered that the ability to delay gratification had a more profound effect than many had originally predicted.

## The Marshmallow Skill

Though the researchers had watched the kids for only a few minutes, what they learned from the experiment was enormously telling. Children who had been able to wait for that second marshmallow matured into adults who were more socially competent, self-assertive, dependable, and capable of dealing with frustrations. They scored an average of 210 points higher on their SATs, got promoted more often, and had happier and more enduring relationships.

Apparently, Mischel had stumbled onto the mother lode of personality traits. The fact that a four-year-old's onetime response to a tempting marshmallow predicts lifelong results is at once exciting and depressing—depending on whether you are a "delayer" or a "grabber."

But is this what's really going on in these studies? Are some people wired to succeed and others to fail? Is the capacity to delay gratification about hardwired motivation or a learnable ability?

In 1965, Dr. Mischel collaborated on a study with Albert Bandura to explore this question.[3] In an experiment similar to the marshmallow studies, the two scholars placed children who had failed to delay gratification into contact with adult role models who knew how to delay. The grabby kids observed adults who avoid picking up the marshmallow by putting their heads down for a nap or getting up from the chair and engaged in some distracting activity. They observed learnable skills for delaying gratification. And to everyone's delight, they followed suit.

After a single exposure to an adult model, children who previously hadn't delayed suddenly became stars at delaying. Even more interesting, in follow-up studies conducted months later, the children who had learned to delay *retained* much of what they had learned during the brief modeling session. It appeared that *will* might be a *skill*.

This is important news to all of us and most certainly offers hope to Henry. When Dr. Mischel took a closer look at individuals who routinely held out for the greater reward, he concluded that delayers are simply more *skilled* at avoiding short-term temptations. They didn't merely avoid the temptation; they employed specific, learnable techniques that kept their attention off what would be merely short-term gratification and on their long-term goal of earning that second marshmallow.

But before any of this is useful to Henry, or the rest of us who are trying to influence positive change, we must first recognize that the three *ability* sources of influence are involved in more ways than we ever imagined in shaping the habits we're after. Your ability to influence change is determined by how well you understand today's behavior.

For example, when you see Lou eating french fries and sending texts on his phone rather than greeting customers, it's tempting to conclude the problem is that Lou is a slug. He is doing what he's doing because he is lazy and self-centered. This is an open-and-shut motivation problem!

But what if there's more going on? What if at least part of the problem is that he feels awkward around customers? What if he lacks social skills? What if he hasn't been well trained in basic cleaning tasks? When you develop the discipline to examine possible ability barriers, you substantially increase your potential for effective influence.

Once Henry understands this, he'll know his life can improve if he learns *skills* for delaying gratification. But will that be enough to transform him into the physically fit person he'd like to become? He considers himself incompetent at all things athletic. Surely factors as hardwired as body type, lung capacity, and musculature are predictors of good athletic performance. Henry has no hope of ever becoming one of those chiseled hunks you see hanging out at health clubs. Right?

## MUCH OF PROWESS IS PRACTICE

Psychologist Anders Ericsson has offered an interesting interpretation of how those at the top of their game get there. After devoting his academic life to learning why some individuals are better at certain tasks than others, Ericsson has repeatedly demonstrated that people who climb to the top eclipse their peers through what he calls *deliberate practice*.[4] And our research shows that this same discipline is a must in an effective influence strategy.

As the saying goes, practice doesn't make perfect; *perfect* practice makes perfect. Ericsson argues there is substantial evidence that people who achieve exceptional performance only get there through carefully guided practice—*perfect* practice.

For instance, Ericsson has described how dedicated figure skaters practice differently on the ice: Olympic hopefuls work on skills they have yet to master. Club skaters, in contrast, work on skills they've already mastered. Amateurs tend to spend *half* of their time at the rink chatting with friends and not practicing at all.

Skaters who spend the same number of hours on the ice achieve very different results because they practice in very different ways. In Ericsson's research, this finding has held true for every skill imaginable, including memorization, chess, violin, public speaking, getting along with others, and holding high-stakes conversations.

Ericsson found that no matter the field of expertise, when it comes to elite status, there is no correlation between time in the profession and performance levels. A 20-year-veteran brain surgeon is not likely to be any more skilled than a 5-year rookie by virtue of time on the job. Any difference between the two has nothing to do with experience and everything to do with deliberate practice.

In this case, surgeons who receive detailed feedback against a known standard develop far more rapidly than colleagues who practice their same old methods over and over again.

Certainly, time is required (most elite performers in fields like music composition, dance, science, fiction writing, chess, and basketball have put in 10 or more years). But time is not the critical variable for mastery. The critical factor is using time wisely. It's the *skill* of practice that makes perfect.

Roger Bacon once said that it would take a person 30 to 40 years to master calculus—the same calculus that is taught in most high schools today. Today's musicians routinely match and even surpass the technical virtuosity of legendary musicians of the past. And when it comes to sports, the records just keep falling. For example, when Johnny Weissmuller of Tarzan fame won his five Olympic gold medals in swimming in 1924, nobody expected that years later *high school* kids would post better times. This was all made possible through deliberate practice.

## What Is Deliberate Practice?

So, what is this all-important discipline of *deliberate practice*? To see it in action, come with us to the top of a 40-meter ski ramp. A 10-year-old girl named Zia stares down the ramp shaking as much with worry as from the cold. Months ago, at Zia's insistence, her mother signed her up to learn ski jumping from former Olympians. It seemed like a great idea at the time. But now, standing on a mountain staring down what appears to be an endless chute, she has doubts.

Yesterday, the first day of ski jumping school, her instructors had her glide effortlessly down a 20-meter ramp. While today's challenge is only 20 meters longer, to Zia the stakes feel much higher. In an attempt to calm herself she says, "I'll be fine. I'll do it. Here goes . . . something . . . I guess." Hearing the tremor in her voice, her coach gives her timely advice: "Just remember, never snowplow. Skis straight. That's all you need to focus on. It's just a longer 20!"

Zia repeats his advice, seizing hold of the reassurance in "It's just a bigger 20! That's all!" Her breath calms and she leans forward to begin her rapid descent. By the time she is 30 meters down she is screaming with exhilaration. "Oh yeah! It's so fun! Sixty seems like nothing now!"

The next day she gets her first air off a 60-meter ramp. After her classmates complete their run, the coach skis to the bottom of the hill where they discuss what happened, then ride to the top for another run.

This brief episode is influence genius. It's a perfect illustration of the three elements of deliberate practice that should be part of any effort to address *ability*. In a few short minutes, this influential coach had his pupils:

1. Practice one or two specific skills
2. At the edge of ability
3. With immediate feedback and coaching

Ericsson's research shows that when these elements are present, skill acquisition accelerates. And when they are absent (which they are in most "learning" settings), very little growth occurs. Here's what that looks like in Zia's case.

## 1. Practice One or Two Specific Skills

The coach doesn't inundate Zia with a dozen skills. He simply says, "Just remember, never snowplow. Skis straight. That's all you need to focus on." He avoids offering the kind of vague abstractions you hear in most learning settings. Little improvement comes from chanting "Be the change you want to see" or "Give 110 percent!"

What people need to build ability is not vacuous philosophy but specific skills.

## 2. Practice Skills at the Edge of Ability

Zia is practicing at the sweet spot for improvement: a bit beyond her current capacity. People learn best under conditions of mild stress. Too much stress shuts down learning, and too little shuts down attention.

## 3. Practice with Immediate Feedback and Coaching

Finally, *immediately* after her performance, the coach tells her what to do differently the next time and *immediately* has her take another run. The more immediate the feedback and next attempt, the more accelerated the learning.

This all might seem obvious for athletic pursuits like ski jumping, but does it apply to an array of workplace behaviors you might want to influence in others? Consider a common problem at hospitals. A surgeon has just committed a medical error. While performing a mastectomy, she has accidentally ripped a tiny muscle guarding the patient's chest cavity, but she doesn't notice her error.

The anesthesiologist sees a gauge jump, so it appears as if one lung is no longer taking in air. Two of the nurses assisting the operation see similar signs of distress. If the medical team doesn't start corrective action soon, the patient could die. But before the action can be taken, either the surgeon needs to take responsibility or one of the other professionals needs to raise an alarm.

Let's focus on the staff members who are assisting and predict what they might do. Most would certainly hesitate to suggest the surgeon made a mistake because if they don't handle the situation well, they'll come off as flippant or even insubordinate. There are legal issues at play, which makes the discussion that much more delicate. Maybe they've seen colleagues who've expressed a concern, turned out to be wrong, and then received a tongue-lashing. Better to let someone else take the risk. Precious seconds continue to pass.

One large healthcare organization decided that this moment was too important to leave to chance. They were dissatisfied to learn that medical mistakes were confronted less than 15 percent of the time by those who witnessed them.[5] So they went to work influencing a new vital behavior of peer accountability. A key to their remarkable improvement was deliberate practice.

They had teams of doctors and nurses practice witnessing errors and speaking up. They developed specific scripts that they would be comfortable delivering, practiced in their working environment with their colleagues, and were given immediate feedback when their approach fell flat. These practice episodes rarely took more than 15 minutes. And in spite of their brevity, those units that used deliberate practice saw substantially more improvement in peer accountability.

## You Can't Change a Life Without Building Skills

There are few better examples of the importance of addressing *ability* as part of an influence effort than The Other Side Academy. The Other Side Academy helps people change their lives by having them practice real skills to solve real problems. And they give them a lot of feedback.

Take Leo. After 6 years of living on the streets and 20 years as a heroin addict, he stumbled into the front door of the Academy and asked for an interview. He was emaciated, dejected, and covered with sores.

Many would argue that those with long criminal histories or patterns of homelessness simply lack motivation. "If they simply wanted to change, they would change" goes the argument. Dave Durocher tells us otherwise: "When our students arrive they know almost nothing about how to live a sober, honest, healthy life. They've honed skills for coping rather than living for decades."

Leo, for example, had never held a job. He was an expert at finding food in dumpsters, navigating homeless service providers, negotiating for drugs, panhandling, avoiding conflict, and dozens of other skills. What he didn't know how to do was get up every day, get along with imperfect people in a workplace, and manage money. That's where living at the Academy came in.

One day Leo was in a peer-coaching meeting when one of his fellow students said, "Leo, you sit like a homeless guy." Academy students don't mince words. At first, Leo was offended. Then he looked at everyone else in the meeting, then at his own sunken abdomen and extended legs. Having recognized the difference, he pulled in his legs, sat up straight, and began acquiring a new set of skills. In subsequent weeks and months, with coaching and feedback from his peers, he learned posture, eye contact, vocabulary, and table manners that suited him well for the life he wanted.

*Learn how a Texas-based furniture company used the Six Sources of Influence to grow revenue, cut expenses and delivery mishaps, and improve employee and customer satisfaction—all during a recession. Read the Gallery Furniture case study at CrucialInfluence.com.*

Let's look at another example of deliberate practice, this time in an office setting. After a disastrously public customer service failure, former Starbucks CEO Howard Schultz recognized the need to help baristas manage the inevitable emotional turbulence of their jobs. On the fateful day, a customer had been brusque with a barista when placing her order. In response, the barista wrote a profanity rather than the usual customer name on the coffee cup.

The story went viral, causing embarrassment and brand damage. Schultz wisely concluded that a lasting solution would take more than simply firing a single employee. He saw the incident as an indication of a lack of skill more than a problem of willful petulance. As evidence, he closed every store in the world for a full day to allow employees to practice new skills for managing these moments of emotional overwhelm.

To see the importance of ability and deliberate practice in influencing change, let's return to the example of the father picking up his 13-year-old from the police station. Following his request for the victim's phone number, Brian was silent for a few minutes. Finally, hanging his head, he said, "Dad, to be honest, when the guys started filling the water balloons, I thought I should say something, but I didn't know what to say."

Now, what did Brian just tell you? Is he describing a motivation or an ability problem? If you aren't careful, you'll classify it as we often do as a motivation problem and offer him a sermon on courage. But that's not what he needs! This is why learning to examine your influence problem through *all* of the sources is so crucial. If you don't, you'll miss perfect moments for appropriate influence.

The father immediately pulled the car once again to the side of the road, turned to his son, and said in playful seriousness, "Son, you're in luck! I'm one of the world's leading experts in Crucial Conversations. And you have me in the car with you!"

Brian rolled his eyes, but continued. "What would you have said, Dad?"

The father offered a possibility that Brian immediately rejected. "They would think I was an idiot if I said that!"

Undeterred, Dad asked Brian, "What would have been better than that?"

Brian chewed his lip for a moment, then burst out with a phrase that Dad thought wasn't especially inspired. He added one suggestion for change, and Brian tried it out.

Brian said, "That would have worked! I totally could have said that, and they would have listened!"

The phrase wasn't anything brilliant, but that didn't matter. All that mattered was whether Brian was willing to take a stand next time he was in a risky situation. So Dad had him rehearse it some more. "OK," Dad said, "Say it again."

He did. Dad had him do it a third time and then asked, "So if you are pressed to do something wrong in the future, will you say that?" Brian pledged to do so. And Dad pulled back onto the road.

Notice what just happened. All the father did was engage Brian in about four minutes of deliberate practice. He practiced a concrete skill, while keeping in mind the stress of the recent episode so the practice would be in realistic conditions. The practice pushed him at the edge of his previous ability. And he got immediate feedback and coaching. But that moment would never have happened had his father not appreciated that he was facing a lack of ability, not simply a motivation problem.

Many of the profound and persistent problems we face stem more from a lack of skill than from a genetic curse, a lack of courage, or a character flaw. Self-discipline and elite performance, long viewed as character traits and genetic gifts, actually result from guided practice of clearly defined skills. Learn how to practice the right actions, and you can master everything from withstanding the temptations of chocolate to holding an awkward discussion with your boss.

**Act Like an Influencer**

The leaders at Newmont Corporation running a gold mine in remote Ghana were trying to reduce automobile accidents by asking their drivers to stop speeding. They discovered most drivers didn't want to speed, but they felt they had to because of an awkward interpersonal situation. They were often asked to drive senior leaders to the airport, a two-hour drive, and these leaders were notorious for cutting it too close. They didn't allow enough time to catch their flights, so their drivers had to speed.

The vital behavior that could solve this problem was for drivers to call the senior leaders an hour in advance to remind them of their scheduled departure time. For the drivers, this was a very awkward and countercultural call to make. It was an ability problem. So they brainstormed scripts they thought could help with more skillful team members. They practiced. They also practiced what they would say when leaders arrived late anyway. Then they invited the safety manager and several senior leaders in for a discussion, where they role-played the conversations with the actual senior leaders who sometimes terrified them.

These role-playing opportunities built both competence and confidence that helped drivers follow through on the vital behavior during very crucial moments.

To hear the rest of the Newmont story, read their case study at CrucialInfluence.com.

## SUMMARY: PERSONAL ABILITY

Changing behavior almost always involves learning new skills. Exceptional leaders make it a priority to engage people in deliberate practice.

If you want to succeed at influence, spend more time engaging people in practicing the new behaviors you want them to enact. Make sure that practice involves:

1. Practice of one or two specific skills
2. At the edge of ability
3. With immediate coaching and feedback

And finally, be sure you help people develop not just the technical, but the interpersonal and *intrapersonal* skills they will need to succeed. Engage them in practice in addressing emotions that might undermine their attempts to change. Help them learn to skillfully move from the *go* to the *know* parts of their brains so they can overcome impulses that might keep them from success.

Remember the good news here. Overcoming bad behaviors or developing complex athletic, intellectual, and interpersonal skills are not merely functions of motivation, personality traits, or even character. They all tie back to ability. Help people develop greater proficiency at deliberate practice, and you will significantly increase your chances for turning new behaviors into long-standing habits.

Our natural tendency is to attribute most negative behavior to motivation problems and almost never consider whether ability is playing a role. If you want to influence change, it's best to do the opposite: consider *ability* problems first, motivation second.

|  | MOTIVATION | ABILITY |
|---|---|---|
| **PERSONAL** | Help Them Love What They Hate | Help Them Do What They Can't |
| **SOCIAL** | **Provide Encouragement** | Provide Assistance |
| **STRUCTURAL** | Reward with Care | Change the Environment |

# 5

# PROVIDE ENCOURAGEMENT

*Source 3: Social Motivation*

---

*We are inescapably shaped by those around us.*

---

No source of influence is more inescapable than source 3, *social motivation*: the persuasive power of the people who make up the social networks of those you hope to lead. None. The ridicule and praise, acceptance and rejection, approval and disapproval of fellow beings can do more to assist or destroy our influence efforts than anything else.

Smart leaders appreciate the tremendous power humans hold over one another, and instead of denying it, lamenting it, or attacking it, they embrace and enlist it. They use the power of social influence to support change by ensuring that the right people provide encouragement, coaching, and even accountability during crucial moments.

## PUSHING PEOPLE PAST THEIR LIMIT

In 1961, psychologist Stanley Milgram set out to find US citizens similar in disposition to what most people believed were the crazy misfits, fundamentalists, and psychological wrecks who had marched Jews, Poles, Romanies, and countless others into the gas chambers at Auschwitz. The world was unnerved by what he discovered.

Mystified by what had happened in Hitler's Germany, Dr. Milgram was interested in what *type* of person could be compelled to annihilate his or her innocent friends and neighbors. Naturally, blind fundamentalists who followed unspeakable orders in the name of political zealotry would be hard to locate in the suburbs of Connecticut. Nevertheless, Milgram was determined to track down a few of them and put them under his microscope.

Of course, Milgram couldn't create circumstances under which his neighbors actually killed each other. But maybe he could trick subjects into *thinking* they were killing someone else. Milgram ran an ad in the New Haven newspaper asking people to take part in an experiment that lasted one hour and for which they would be paid $4.50.[1] Interested people reported to the basement of Linsly-Chittenden Hall on the campus of Yale University. They were told they were taking part in a study that examined the impact of negative reinforcement on learning.

While waiting for their turn to earn $4.50, subjects chatted with another participant about the upcoming job. This friendly stranger was actually a confederate of Dr. Milgram's who was working as part of the research team.

Next, a scientist in a lab jacket would appear and ask each of the two participants to reach into a bowl and draw out a slip of paper to determine who would perform which of the two jobs in the study. One would be a teacher, and one would be a learner.

In actuality, both slips said "teacher," guaranteeing that the actual research subject would take the role of the teacher.

The teacher accompanied the learner and the researcher into a small booth where the learner was invited to sit down while the researcher applied special paste to his arms. "This," he explained, "is to ensure solid contact between your skin and the electrodes when we administer the shocks."

At this point, the learner explained, "A few years ago in the veterans' hospital I was told I had a bit of a heart condition. Will that be a problem?" To which the researcher confidently said, "No. While the shocks may be painful, they are not dangerous."

After strapping the electrodes to the learner, the researcher closed the booth door and took the teacher (the subject) to an adjoining room. There the teacher would see a frightening piece of electrical machinery with which he or she would deliver shocks to the learner. To reassure subjects that the machine was pumping out real electrons, each teacher would be given a 45-volt burst from the machine as a sample of the initial shock the learner in the other room would receive during the experiment. It hurt.

Again, the researcher explained that the reason for administering shocks was to measure the impact of negative reinforcement on learning. The teacher was told to read a list of paired words loud enough for the learner to hear in the adjoining room. The teacher then read the first word in each pair, and the learner tried to recall the second word. If the learner got the word wrong, the teacher threw a switch that shocked the poor learner with the supposed heart problems. With each subsequent missed word, the teacher flipped another switch, administering a higher voltage and a more painful shock.

Of course, the learner wasn't actually being shocked. Instead, with each increase in voltage, the researcher played a prerecorded audio clip that the subject could hear through the wall. With the first shock came a grunt. The second shock produced a mild protest. Next, stronger protests. Then screaming and shouting. Then screaming and banging on the wall with a reminder that he had heart problems. Eventually, when the voltage levels exceeded 315 volts, the teacher heard nothing but silence as he or she read the words, raised the voltage, and flipped the switch.

Milgram suspected he would have to experiment with a lot of subjects before he'd find anyone who would proceed past 315 volts. In fact, when Milgram asked a sample group of psychologists to predict the results of this study, they suggested that only 1.2 percent of the population, only a "sadistic few," would give the maximum voltage.

When you watch black-and-white film clips of Milgram's actual subjects taking part in the study, the hair stands up on the back of your neck. At first these everyday folks off the streets of Connecticut chuckle nervously as they hear the learner grunt in protest after being given a 45-volt shock. Some show signs of stress as they increase the voltage and the learner starts to shout. Many pause at around 135 volts and question the purpose of the experiment.

If at any time the subjects called for a halt, the scientist in the white lab jacket said that the experiment required them to continue—up to four times. If subjects requested to stop a fifth time, the experiment stopped. Otherwise, the experiment came to an end only after the subject had given the maximum 450 volts—to a learner who was no longer responding—giving the teacher the distinct impression that the learner had either passed out or died.

Clearly the subjects who continued to send more and more volts took no pleasure in what they were doing. It's unnerving to watch clips as anguished subjects suggest that they should stop the torture. But when told by a person in a white lab coat to continue, they comply. And not in the low numbers Milgram and hundreds of psychologists predicted.

As it turned out, 65 percent of subjects continued to 450 volts. In another version of the experiment, Milgram paired subjects with another confederate playing the role of a fellow teacher who appeared to blithely go along with instructions. Under this condition, *90 percent of subjects reached 450 volts.*

Dr. Milgram hadn't discovered a tiny handful of Connecticut zealots who would gladly give their souls over to the totalitarian cause as he expected. He had found the vulnerable target within all of us. He had looked for the sadistic few and found himself—and you and me.

## THE POWER OF SOCIAL INFLUENCE

Decades of experiments in social psychology make one thing clear: we are inescapably shaped by those around us. We are hardwired to look to others for *affirmation*, *information*, *inspiration*, and *association*. While this human tendency accounts for tremendous human achievements, Milgram's experiment, provoked by Nazi genocide, gives a dire warning of how this source of influence can be used for ill purposes. Our craving for *affirmation*, our willingness to unthinkingly consume *information* from dubious experts, and our hunger to *belong* can be used to manipulate us in horrifying ways. But the right response of leaders to these cautions is not to avoid, but to embrace the positive use of social influence. If those leading positive change fail to profit from social influence, they cede its power to those with lesser motives.

Great leaders ensure that people feel praised, emotionally supported, and encouraged by those around them every time they enact vital behaviors. And they ensure that people feel discouraged or even socially sanctioned when they make the wrong choice.

Our decades of studying social change taught us three things about social influence:

1. Social influence starts with you. No influence effort can succeed if the leader doesn't "walk the talk."
2. The pace of change is determined by how quickly formal leaders and opinion leaders join in.
3. Peer accountability is the ultimate accelerant for change.

Let's take a look at how each of these findings can help you harness the power of social motivation.

## IT STARTS WITH YOU

We once watched a striking example of social influence. The CEO of a large defense contractor, whom we'll call Ken, was trying to transform a rather timid culture into one in which individuals openly stated their differing opinions to resolve long-standing problems.

After months of lecturing, Ken faced a crucial moment. In a meeting of his top 200 managers, he extended an invitation. "I've been told that I'm unapproachable," he began. "I am trying to work on it. But to be honest, I don't know what it means entirely. I'd appreciate feedback from any of you who would be willing to help me."

For a few seconds, the auditorium felt like a morgue. As Ken scanned the audience for any takers, he was about to break the awkward silence and move on to a new topic when a woman named Shirley raised her hand. "Sure, Ken. I've got some suggestions."

With that announcement, Ken set an appointment to talk one-on-one with Shirley. As you might guess, from that moment on most of the water-cooler chatter was about the foolish risk Shirley had just taken. Pay-per-view could have made a fortune selling access to the private meeting between Ken and Shirley. But in the end, the entire story came out—from Ken.

After meeting with Shirley (and with Shirley's permission) Ken sent out an email detailing the feedback he'd received. Just as importantly, Ken sincerely thanked Shirley for her candor. He finished by making commitments to a couple of changes he hoped would make him more approachable, and he followed through.

In this instance, Ken showed genuine support of candor by sincerely listening to the person who had taken the risk to be honest, and he then made personal changes to demonstrate his commitment. His actions demonstrated his willingness to walk the talk, and the results were far-reaching. Within months, candor among employees increased measurably across the entire organization. Employees began to open up and successfully solve problems.

What was it about this single incident that amplified its influence? First, the leader led. Second, an opinion leader helped. And third, the two of them created a memorable vicarious experience for the other 199 managers.

Shirley's role was crucial. But the first ingredient of success was the leader. It all begins with you. Notice also that the vital behavior Ken advocated conflicted with people's past perception of him. And yet in spite of that, this pivotal moment influenced remarkable change. Let's examine how.

## Act Like an Influencer

A nurse manager begins staff meetings by sharing "the good, the bad, and the ugly" of what has happened during the last week. She usually begins with her own observations. In so doing, she models that it's safe to share bad news and failures, without any sugarcoating.

When others take the risk to share challenges and setbacks they've experienced, she responds with appreciation: "That's a great observation!" "Thanks for noticing that!" Her reactions show that it's safe to speak honestly. The team then uses these stories of failures and successes to improve future care.

## Lead the Way

The first place to look for social influence is in the mirror. When you ask people to take on new behaviors, the first question they ask is, "Why should I follow *you*?" When you ask people to change, many of the new behaviors are far more physically or emotionally challenging than what's required to maintain the status quo. You're asking people to step from a familiar, comfortable action into a world of uncertainty or difficulty.

Muhammad Siddiqui (top right) sacrificed time
to connect with opinion leaders in their homes.

For example, we worked with Mohammad Siddiqui, CEO of the South Sudan affiliate of telecommunications and digital services giant MTN. When Siddiqui took the job, he inherited a pretty cynical workforce. Due to political unrest and economic upheaval, local currency had lost 85 percent of its value. Thus, his workforce was living on 85 percent less than it had a year before. In addition, employees saw management as unsympathetic and demanding.

Employee engagement and productivity were unacceptably low. Siddiqui was under pressure to dramatically improve results. He knew he would need the full intellectual engagement of his employees in order to make progress. So he started an effort to foster a new vital behavior. He wanted all employees to "speak up irrespective of the level or position of the person you need to address."

His employees were stunned. First, because this was counter to the country's culture. In South Sudan there is a strict sense of propriety about who speaks to whom—much less who *disagrees* with whom. And second, here was the man they partly associated with their unsatisfactory wages. He had explained that the company would not survive if it gave substantial across-the-board pay increases. And now he was asking his employees to behave in ways that were terribly uncomfortable—even risky. Not a chance. They saw the invitation as a trick, a way of pretending to address employee concerns with no sacrifice from management.

When you ask people to step into a place of uncertainty and change, they look to you to take their cues. They look at your behavior. Unfortunately, they have a bias for interpreting your behavior in ways that confirm rather than deny their existing concerns or mistrust. To encourage them to change, you have to generate clear, unambiguous evidence that they can believe you. But how?

## Sacrifice Breathes Life into Dead Values

Many people believe that the only way to build social influence is to slowly build a relationship of trust with those you lead. "Give it time" is the mantra. But such a belief is an influence death sentence for someone like Siddiqui. He was a new CEO, from another country no less, who needed to influence change today—not five years from now.

Fortunately, as we saw with Ken, the "give it time" theory is largely wrong. Within months Siddiqui built so much social influence with his team that behavior began to change in remarkable ways. What did he do to make his stated beliefs both clear and credible—in an environment where people could draw negative conclusions about anything he did? Siddiqui learned that making a *sacrifice* can be a powerful influence accelerant.

The first thing Siddiqui did was unprecedented in South Sudanese culture. He listened and apologized. In public discussions with employees, he listened carefully and attended to the pain they were experiencing due to the massive depreciation of their currency. He empathized with their plight, brainstormed ways he could help soften the blow, but ultimately explained that if the company was to remain viable (and they were to keep their jobs), there was little he could do.

However, as employees left these candid sessions, more than one remarked that this was the first time they had ever heard a leader quietly, humbly, and sincerely say the words "I am sorry." Something inside them began to stir.

Siddiqui didn't stop there. One weekend Siddiqui and his seven-year-old daughter visited the home of Jafar (not his real name)—a well-respected MTN employee. Jafar, positioned 10 levels below Siddiqui in the job of janitor, was stunned when the big boss and his daughter called and asked to visit. At the appointed time, Siddiqui arrived. He paid homage to the home. He warmly greeted Jafar's father and mother, who lived with Jafar. He inquired about Jafar's circumstances. He expressed gratitude for Jafar's long service and promised to do his best as a leader to earn his trust.

Each weekend Siddiqui paid similar visits to other employees from throughout the organization. In a matter of months, the talk about Siddiqui's invitations to change were no longer ridiculed. The widespread view was that this was a man they could trust. A man who *deserved* their support.

If you want to increase your influence with those you hope to help change—knowing full well that others can simply discount your speeches or misinterpret your actions—you're going to have to make some *sacrifices*. You must regularly demonstrate your sincerity by generating indisputable evidence that you believe in what you say. You say that openness is important and then sacrifice pride to prove your point.

MTN employees had seen generations of leaders who valued being held in high esteem (even being deferred to) above all else. Bosses are important. Then along came a man who was willing to sacrifice his own pride and be treated as a peer. He called for openness and candid dialogue. He listened. He apologized. He entered humble homes. This was a man who walked the talk.

Let's take a look at four kinds of sacrifices that can act as a trust accelerant in your influence efforts: time, money, ego, and other priorities.

## Time

Siddiqui's behavior was remarkable because it illustrated sacrifice on many levels. One of the most compelling sacrifices was with his time. When people heard about his personal visits to employees' homes, they wanted details. They wanted to know what he said. How he behaved. Where he sat. But also, how long he stayed.

We all know time is a finite commodity. No one has any more of it than anyone else. No one has found a way to create more of it. So we trust that it is a credible demonstration of our values.

Had Siddiqui made a brief and effusive five-minute visit, it would have sent an entirely different message than his hour-long conversation over tea did to everyone. If you want to persuade people that you are serious, sacrifice your time.

## Money

We (the authors) became loyal customers of the car rental company Hertz after 9/11. Two of us were in Dallas, Texas, on business when the attack came. Since all aircraft were grounded indefinitely, we were left with no way to get home to our worried families. We placed a call to Hertz to ask how much it would cost to drive the rented car the 2,500 miles from Dallas to Salt Lake City. The agent replied, "Nothing. We've got this. You take the car wherever you need to go. You get home to your family. Turn it in at the most convenient Hertz location. There will be no drop-off fee. Take care." We were speechless.

We knew that Hertz talked about customer service. Its ads were full of such ideas. Now we believed that it actually did care about customers. Why? Because the company took a huge hit to the bottom line (at least in the short run) to do what was best to serve its customers in a time of crisis. Anyone who sacrifices money to serve customers cares about customers.

## Ego

You're going to screw up. There will be times that you behave in ways that are opposite of the vital behaviors you hope to foster. But this isn't the end of the world. In fact, it can be a powerful opportunity for you to enhance trust by sacrificing ego.

We once worked with a leader we'll call Liz. Liz was a facility manager in Kuala Lumpur. Her campaign to improve quality screeched to a halt one day at the end of a manager briefing when she responded to questions written on cards from the 200-person audience. One comment read, "Yesterday you and the execs from Japan were supposed to do a facility tour. My team spent all weekend preparing for the tour and you never showed up." Liz's face turned red. She slapped the card down on the rostrum. She removed her glasses, then said, "Yesterday I had a decision to make. I had to decide whether to spend two hours with our senior executives touring the facility, or discuss the future of the company. I chose the latter and would do the same today. Next question?" The session ended quite uncomfortably.

Liz was immediately repentant. She knew she had just damaged trust. She knew she had violated her own vital behaviors (which didn't include putting someone down in a meeting and becoming righteously indignant). Fortunately, it all changed the next week during a similar briefing. As Liz began, she stepped from behind the podium. She bowed her head. And she said with some emotion. "Last week I behaved despicably." She went on to describe what had happened. Then concluded with, "I beg your forgiveness. That was unacceptable. And I will not do that again." And she didn't.

Ironically, the apology had a more powerful effect on trust than if she had behaved perfectly in the previous meeting. In that moment of public contrition her team learned that her espoused value of openness and respect were more important than her ego.

A mistake or two is not the end of the world—so long as you demonstrate what matters most by sacrificing ego to integrity.

## Other Priorities

There was a time when some employees at Lockheed Martin Aeronautics wrongly concluded that their CEO, Dain Hancock, was all about image. That he cared more about impressing outsiders than about attending to employee needs—including listening to what they had to say.

This changed one day when Dain was holding an employee feedback meeting. Fifteen minutes into the 90-minute session his secretary rushed in to announce: "The prince is here two hours early."

Visiting royalty was scheduled to arrive following the session to discuss a multibillion-dollar order of F-16s. Dain paused. Every employee in the room would have understood if he had canceled the session. Instead, Dain assigned his COO to bring his apologies and greet the prince. Dain's decision to continue the feedback session over attending to the prince took mere minutes to ripple across the 13,000-person facility. By sacrificing what people had previously perceived to be his priority (impressing outsiders), Dain's stated value of listening to others gained enormous credibility and went a long way in encouraging others to do the same.

———

The first responsibility for creating social support for change lies in your own actions. Nothing makes a new vital behavior seem more credible than when you sacrifice time, money, ego, and other priorities to demonstrate that what you *say* is important to you really *is* important to you.

## ENGAGE FORMAL AND OPINION LEADERS

We've seen that one person, especially a formal leader, can have an enormous effect on motivating others to enact vital behaviors. If you want to influence change, it's essential that you engage the chain of command.

Smart leaders spend a disproportionate amount of time with formal leaders to ensure that they use their social influence to encourage vital behaviors. They develop specific plans for formal leaders to regularly teach, model, praise, and hold people accountable for behaving in new and better ways.

But there's a second, often overlooked, group of people whose social support or resistance will make or break your influence efforts. To find out who this group is and how to enlist it, let's take a look at the work of Dr. Everett Rogers. His contribution to influence theory has important implications for how all parents, coaches, and business leaders can use social support.

After graduating with a PhD in sociology and statistics, Dr. Rogers took a job with the local university extension service. It was his responsibility to encourage Iowa farmers to use new and improved strains of corn. The new strains produced greater yields and were dramatically more disease resistant, and therefore far more profitable than current strains. What could be easier?

At first, Dr. Rogers figured his job would be easy. He had made a careful study of the crops farmers should grow. He was now working for the experts in agronomy. He figured that when he talked, farmers would be taking notes and thanking him for helping them increase their yields.

But it didn't work that way. As Rogers talked with local farmers about the terrific new seeds he was recommending, he quickly learned that his education and connection to the university didn't impress them. He wasn't exactly one of them.

Dr. Rogers wasn't just different. In the farmers' view, he was the wrong kind of different. He had never plowed a field. Sure, he said he read books, but what if he was wrong? Who would dare put their annual harvest at risk by listening to a young fellow just out of college? None of the farmers, that's who.

After being rejected by his target population, Rogers grew desperate. What good is it to invent better methods if no one will put them into practice? The very advance of civilization relies on citizens letting go of old, inefficient ways and embracing new, efficient ones. And Rogers just happened to know what those better ways were—at least for the farmers.

What could Rogers do if people wouldn't listen to *him*? Perhaps, he concluded, he could get a farmer to embrace the new strains of corn. If a person from within the farming community could point to the better results, everyone would be happy to follow.

He found one willing participant. This particular farmer was very open-minded. He was also a rather hip fellow who wore Bermuda shorts and drove a Cadillac. He had a proclivity for embracing innovation. He tried the new strains of corn and enjoyed a bumper crop. But no one cared. The next season, not one additional farmer planted even an acre of the new strain.

Apparently this willing farmer was also too much of an outsider to have strong influence in the wider group.

This unvarnished failure changed the course of Rogers's life. He spent the rest of his career learning what happens to innovations as they move through a social system.

## Opinion Leaders Versus Early Adopters

Dr. Rogers was shocked to discover that the merit of an idea did not predict its adoption rate. Instead, what predicted whether an innovation was widely accepted or not was whether a specific group of people embraced it. Period.

Rogers learned that the first people to latch on to a new idea are unlike the masses in many ways. He called these people "innovators." They're the ones in the Bermuda shorts. They tend to be more well-informed on and open to new ideas. But here's the important point. The key to getting the majority of any population to adopt a vital behavior is to find out who these innovators are *and avoid them like the plague.* If they are the only ones who embrace your new idea, it will die.

The second group to try an innovation is made up of what Dr. Rogers termed "early adopters." Many early adopters are what are commonly known as "opinion leaders." These important people represent about 13.5 percent of the population. They are also more well-informed, and they tend to be open to new ideas. But they are different from innovators in one critical respect: they are socially *connected* and *respected.* The rest of the population—over 85 percent—will not adopt the new practices *until opinion leaders do.*

When the fellow with the Bermuda shorts used the new seeds, he didn't do Rogers a favor. Cadillac man was an *innovator.* He was the first to adopt new ideas in his community, and like many innovators, his adoption cast suspicion on the new ways he endorsed. Since he was different from the majority of his peers in visible ways, and since much of what he did appeared to disrespect traditional methods, this made him a threat. He was neither respected nor connected. And thus, no one else bought in.

Great leaders we studied routinely use this powerful source of influence. For example, when Dr. Don Berwick and IHI try to influence the behavior of hundreds of thousands of physicians across the United States, they first engage the *guilds,* as they call them. These are the associations and research groups other physicians look to as credible sources. When the guilds talk, physicians listen.

Likewise, Dr. Donald Hopkins and his team at The Carter Center don't consider going into a Guinea worm–affected village without first working with the village chief or drawing on the power of a respected official. These formal leaders identify respected village members from different groups or clans who will be listened to when they teach people the vital behaviors for eradicating Guinea worm disease.

"The message," Hopkins says, "is no more important than the messenger."

Opinion leaders can be influential even when they aren't real. The TV and radio heroes in Tanzania we referred to earlier *become* opinion leaders. For example, in the village of Lutsaan, India, a community action group made a solemn covenant to educate their daughters after listening to the wildly popular show *Tinka, Tinka Sukh* ("Happiness Lies in Small Things"). In this poignant TV drama, a beloved young girl dies in childbirth after being forced into an early marriage. After vicariously experiencing her death, audience members wrote over 150,000 letters in reaction to the episode. Listeners were so affected by what happened to the young girl that 184 Lutsaan villagers placed their thumbprints on a large public poster in honor of their fallen heroine in a gesture of solidarity and support.

"Of course I will not marry off my daughter before she turns 18," one listener told Dr. Arvind Singhal, who was commissioned to study the effects of the serial drama. "Prior to listening to *Tinka, Tinka Sukh*, I had it in my mind that I need to marry off my daughter soon. Now I won't, and I tell others as well."

*Tinka, Tinka Sukh* made double use of opinion leaders by ending each episode with an epilogue during which a respected real person from the community asked questions, made a call to action, and encouraged public discourse.

### Act Like an Influencer

At one of Danny Meyer's restaurants, a server was asked by a customer if he knew where he could buy a good cigar along Madison Avenue. The server responded that, while he didn't know the answer to *that*, he *did* know one of the restaurant's staff had just returned from Puerto Rico and had a great "stash" himself. The server returned with the colleague seconds later and presented the guest with a gift of a fine cigar, pausing for a moment to tell about the family from which it was procured and the loving details about its preparation.

On hearing of this "hospitality legend," Danny invited the skillful server to become a mentor. Mentors are chosen from respected opinion leaders and then paired with newer employees to train them in the values and norms of Union Square Hospitality Group. Danny uses valued opinion leaders to encourage the vital behaviors that make his restaurants extraordinary.

Going back to the corporate world, we once watched a remarkable example of opinion leader engagement in Dubai. Jyoti Desai, a telecom CEO, was intent on breaking down silos and encouraging more inter-business unit collaboration. To jump-start change, she carefully identified opinion leaders from every area of the organization and invited them to a three-day retreat alongside her entire management team.

Part of the retreat involved a candid 90-minute conversation between her executive team—seated at the front of the room—and opinion leaders. The topic: "What behaviors will executives need to change if we want others to truly break down silos?" Feedback was fast and furious. At the end, executives created a "Leadership Contract" with opinion leaders, where they committed to six behaviors they would change within themselves.

At the end of the process, Jyoti and her team signed the flipchart listing the six behaviors. She then stood in front of the group and said, "We will make these changes. And when we do, can we count on you to teach this new way of working to others?" The response was a spontaneous ovation. And subsequent behavior change across the company was equally impressive.

Jyoti Desai's willingness to sacrifice ego in candid dialogue with opinion leaders earned her rapid support.

Dr. Everett Rogers's discovery offers enormous influence leverage. When it comes to creating change, you don't have to worry about influencing everyone at once. If you preside over a company with 10,000 employees, your job is to find the 500 or so opinion leaders who are the key to everyone else. If you supervise 20 people, odds are 2 or 3 of them hold more sway over the team than others. Spend more time with them. Listen to their concerns. Build trust with them. Be open to their ideas. Rely on them to share your ideas, and you'll gain a source of influence unlike any other.

## HOW TO FIND OPINION LEADERS

You don't get to decide whether or not you engage the help of opinion leaders. By definition, they will always be engaged. They always observe and judge your leadership strategy—that's what they do. Then they will give your ideas either a thumbs-up or a thumbs-down in their informal interactions with others. They will exert their widely felt influence and decide the destiny of your strategy—whether you like it or not.

If you're interested in engaging opinion leaders in a large organization, the good news is that finding them is quite easy. Since opinion leaders are employees who are most admired and connected to others in the organization, simply ask people to make a list of the employees who they believe are the most influential and respected. Then gather the lists and identify those who are named most frequently. These are the opinion leaders. Once you know who they are, enlist them and partner with them in your efforts to institute change.

> *One of the world's oldest miners and producers of gold needed to improve safety. They started by getting opinion leaders on board with the change efforts. Read the Gold Fields case study at CrucialInfluence.com to see how well they did.*

## ENLIST PEER ACCOUNTABILITY

One of the greatest barriers to any change project lies in unhealthy norms. When you see behavior that is bad but everyone else sees it as normal, you're in deep trouble. You can muster every other source of influence to resist long-standing norms—but you're still likely to fail in your effort to create change unless you take direct action to create *a new sense of normal*.

But there's good news in this as well. Once you foster new norms, change becomes almost inevitable—raising the question: How do you create new norms?

Here's how:

1. Make the undiscussable discussable.
2. Create 200 percent accountability.

## Make the Undiscussable Discussable

Unhealthy norms are almost always sustained by a culture of silence. For example, we found a terrible code of silence when conducting a multiyear study of healthcare in the United States, Thailand, Australia, and the United Kingdom. We began this study to discover why hundreds of thousands of patients contract infections *while in the hospital.*[2]

When we asked neonatology nurses and doctors how infections find their way into the pristine environment of a neonatal unit, people would lower their voices, look both ways, and relate very similar stories. First was the story of physicians who periodically failed to gown up, glove up, or wash up as they should. Second was the story of nurses who, when starting an IV on a very tiny baby, would cut a hole in their sterile gloves to expose a fingertip. The nurses had a good reason for doing this. It's extremely hard to find a vein on a baby who can fit in the palm of your hand. Nevertheless, exposing the finger was a violation of safety practices and sometimes spread infections to vulnerable babies.

The problem in this particular hospital was not merely that a doctor or nurse broke rules. The problem was that there was a conspiracy of silence that kept people from speaking when colleagues violated hygiene, safety, or any other protocol. The existing social norm called for silence. It stated that deferring to power players (like doctors or nurse managers) was more important than protecting patients.

Nothing would ever change in these organizations until the norm changed. Speaking up had to become as normal as donning scrubs.

We have poked around in every type of organization imaginable over the years, and we have found this same code of silence that sustains unhealthy behavior in every corner of business and government.

For instance, we conducted an international study of project management where we explored the colossal failure rates of major high-stakes projects, programs, and initiatives.

We knew from the outset that the vast majority of product launches, reorganizations, mergers, and improvement initiatives either fail or grossly disappoint. Roughly 90 percent of major projects violate their own schedules, budgets, or quality standards.

So we searched for the cause behind these embarrassing results. We learned that 88 percent of those we surveyed were currently working on projects or initiatives that they predicted would eventually fail—yet they continued to plod along.

Then we learned the reason behind the reason: *fewer than 1 in 10 respondents said that it was politically acceptable to speak openly about what was going wrong.* Most suggested that problems such as weak sponsorship, unreasonable constraints, or uncommitted team members were eventually going to kill their efforts, but they said no one—including the project managers themselves—could bring the issues out into the open.

The first step to changing norms is breaking the code of silence that *always* sustains the status quo. When you make the undiscussable discussable, you openly embrace rather than fight the power of social influence. Changes in behavior must be preceded by changes in the public discourse.

To see how to take this first step toward creating new norms, let's return to the Indian village of Lutsaan and revisit the mechanism through which the radio drama *Tinka, Tinka Sukh* affected public opinion. Although the villagers weren't facing hospital infections or failed projects, they did run into a powerful social norm that caused many of them great pain, and their problem was completely undiscussable.

The villagers went from silence around lack of education and early marriage to openly committing to change. What brought about this tremendous change in norms?

According to Dr. Arvind Singhal, the power of the show stemmed from its ability to force an undiscussable topic into the public discourse. Long-settled beliefs were suddenly opened to question and discussed at every corner, workstation, and shop—and eventually reshaped.

Before the episodes aired, millions of people had placed pressure on their friends, children, and coworkers to continue to honor the traditions of their past. This was peer pressure at its strongest. Some people had already changed their views on the treatment of young girls, but it was difficult for them to share their views openly without falling victim to public ridicule. Many people were uncertain about the tradition and wanted to be able to talk it through, but once again, it just wasn't done.

Leaders applied the power of stories (vicarious experience) to the issue. They didn't preach the evils of the traditional treatment of girls because, as we all know, verbal persuasion typically leads to resistance. But the leaders didn't back away either. Instead, they created a serial drama containing likable characters who talked about the social problem in the privacy of their home—while thousands listened in. The beloved family discussed the pros and cons of the tradition, and each show ended with the words of a respected narrator who merely asked questions.

As the radio family experienced its tragedy, family members began talking. They helped others first think about the issues and then talk about them with their friends, coworkers, neighbors, and family. As a result, an undiscussable became a discussable, and what had remained underground for centuries wilted in the light of public discourse.

We've seen the same strategy work to reshape norms in organizations. For example, in one world-renowned academic hospital, leaders were struggling to engage their legendary physician leaders in improving the quality of patient care. Most seemed focused on *learning* about disease but seemed to care little about *treating people* who had diseases. And yet no one would admit it publicly.

This all changed one weekend when we presented the chief medical officer with a stack of 50 patient horror stories we had collected.

She told us later, "When I returned home Friday night, I poured myself a glass of wine, sat in my reading chair, and read the first story. Three hours and 50 stories later I was emotionally overcome."

Beginning Monday morning, what had formerly been undiscussable became widely discussed. The stories were shared, read, and studied. What had been formerly only whispered was now openly debated. As the chief medical officer broke the code of silence, her formerly complacent organization took the first determined step toward change.

If you want to change an old norm, you have to talk about the old norm. You have to talk about the new norm. You have to talk.

## Create 200 Percent Accountability

The pace of change is determined by the speed with which you can get everyone to hold everyone accountable. Whether through encouragement of the right behavior, confronting the wrong behavior, or a combination of the two, the strength of new norms is dependent on the consistency with which people are willing to speak up and defend them.

No one knows—or shows—this better than Dave Durocher. It's semester break at The Other Side Academy. All 150 residents in the Salt Lake City campus have gathered in the family room where they quietly jostle and joke with one another. There's an air of excitement. After all, it's graduation day. This means that some of the students are about to advance to more responsible positions. Others will move to a new job. Younger students may be ready to graduate from freshman, where the requirements are pretty basic. But the accomplishment will be no less celebrated than that of the person who is about to become a senior leader.

So here the students sit, waiting for graduation to begin. Those who haven't been through the ceremony before look terribly uncomfortable. They know they will be singled out in front of hundreds of peers and guests, and they have no clue how to deal with the moment. Then their names are called. They stand up and are given a crisp green sophomore shirt and a beautiful new pair of tennis shoes. They are told that they have done good work and are now assigned to food services. Congratulations!

Tori Dixon, a student at The Other Side Academy,
advances as a leader by learning to hold others accountable.

All of a sudden, these new students hear a sound that has never before been directed at them. Everyone is clapping for them.

"It's the most wonderful time," says Durocher. "They're crying. Huge clapping. You'll see this huge guy who doesn't know what to do with his arms because he's so uncomfortable. And it's the best thing in the world."

So what's going on here? Dave knows how to gain an upper hand over his number one enemy. The illegal, immoral, and antisocial behavior the students formerly engaged in required a strong social system to support it. Criminals run in packs. The distinctly different and healthy behavior that the Academy will demand of each new student requires an even stronger social system. So that's precisely what Dave serves up. The Other Side Academy immerses residents in a whole new culture composed of healthy expectations.

One of the Academy's vital behaviors is "200 percent accountability"—for everyone to challenge everyone. This means that from day one students are hit by an unrelenting wave of social praise and social punishment. Durocher has gone to great pains to structure positive and negative peer feedback into every moment of everyday life. And since the feedback comes from people who have lived the same life, it's hard for new students to dismiss the data.

From day one, those arriving from jail or the streets are told they will be expected to do three things: pull others up, pass information, and play The Game. "Pull ups" are verbal corrections given by anyone to anyone. Every student is expected to give brief verbal correction to anyone they see violating a norm. Second, they are instructed to "pass information"—meaning that after either being pulled up or pulling someone else up, they are to notify their immediate supervisor (who is just an older peer leader in the house). And finally, twice a week, they play "Games." Games is a two-hour-long group feedback process where students express their concerns with one another in greater detail. They practice breathtaking candor, helping one another become aware of and address their moral weaknesses.

For example, in a recent session of Games one student let another know she resented his staring at the women in the house. He flushed red and denied the claim until other men confirmed her observation. He left humbled and more circumspect about his behavior. Another pointed out how his teammate on the moving company seemed to carry pillows when others were carrying heavy furniture. He resolved to be a better teammate. Others were counseled by peers about lying, isolating, surliness, and bigotry.

The sophisticated moral reasoning of these sessions is not only striking given the background of the participants, but humbling to any who participate. Freshmen experience a kind of social whiplash as they discover that norms at the Academy are more than just words on a wall, but are ironclad expectations of everyone in the house. The speed with which social norms change is not a function of time; it is a function of the speed with which peers speak up when they're violated.

This is the secret of the Academy's success. Ensure that everyone understands that they are not just 100 percent accountable—but 200 percent accountable. Create an environment in which everyone is responsible not just to *enact* the vital behaviors themselves—but to *hold others accountable* for them as well.

New norms take hold the instant people begin to defend them. When a critical mass of people practice 200 percent accountability, change is all but assured.

## SUMMARY: SOCIAL MOTIVATION

People who are respected and connected can exert an enormous amount of influence over any change effort. Under stressful and ambiguous circumstances, a mere glance from someone who is considered to be a respected official can be enough to influence people to act in novel ways.

1. **It starts with you.** When a vital behavior is difficult or unpopular, you must lead the way. You must not just talk the talk—you have to walk it as well. People aren't likely to trust your words until you demonstrate your willingness to sacrifice old values for new ones. You'll need to create visible and believable evidence by sacrificing time, money, ego, and other priorities before people will take similar risks themselves.

2. **Engage formal and opinion leaders.** You will also need the support of people with more immediate contact with those you're trying to influence. The support of formal leaders and opinion leaders make it safe for people to embrace innovation. Learn how to identify and partner with these important people.

3. **Enlist peer accountability.** Finally, sometimes change efforts call for changes in widely shared norms. You can't change norms without discussing them; so first, make it safe to talk about high-stakes and controversial topics. Second, to create new norms, invite everyone to hold everyone else accountable. Create a widely shared norm of 200 percent accountability— where everyone is responsible not just to practice the new behaviors, but to communicate clear expectations to everyone else.

Social influence, the deeply felt desire to be accepted, respected, and connected to other human beings, sits at the top of the heap of all sources of influence. Learn how to tap into the power of social influence, and you can change just about anything.

Decades of experiments in social psychology make one thing clear: we are inescapably shaped by those around us. We are hardwired to look to others for affirmation, information, inspiration, and association. Great leaders not only "walk the talk," but they also ensure people feel praised, emotionally supported, and encouraged by those around them.

|            | MOTIVATION                          | ABILITY                        |
| ---------- | ----------------------------------- | ------------------------------ |
| PERSONAL   | Help Them Love What They Hate       | Help Them Do What They Can't   |
| SOCIAL     | Provide Encouragement               | **Provide Assistance**         |
| STRUCTURAL | Reward with Care                    | Change the Environment         |

# 6

# PROVIDE ASSISTANCE

## *Source 4: Social Ability*

---

*Those around us form the "social capital" of our lives—the*
*human resources that help us surpass our individual limits.*

---

As we saw in the previous chapter, most of our actions are far more influenced by others than many of us imagine. That's why great leaders take care to ensure that those they want to influence are sufficiently *encouraged* to adopt vital behaviors. But encouragement isn't enough. Offering a supportive smile is good, but when people need permission, information, coaching, or hands-on help, a friendly nod won't cut it. Instead, you'll need to engage source 4, *social ability*.

## EXAMPLE: ENGAGING SOCIAL ABILITY IN GRASSROOTS ENTREPRENEURSHIP

We'll start this chapter with an example from one of the most remarkable leaders we've ever met, Muhammad Yunus. His influence has extended to hundreds of millions across the globe. One of whom is Tanika, whom we'll introduce first.

Seated in a tight circle in a neat, tin-roofed building in a small village in central India, we find five women—Tanika, Kamara, Damini, Payal, and Sankul. They're in the middle of the most important meeting they'll ever attend. They're selecting the businesses they'll start through small loans from Grameen Bank, a microcredit firm that has set up shop in the region.

Even though none of these women has ever held a job outside the home or taken a single course in business, and even though all are caring for their families with little or no help from their husbands or ex-husbands, nobody will tell these five women what businesses to start. They will invent businesses on their own.

Today each of the other women in this circle will offer feedback to Tanika about her business plan. She is desperate to get started because, like many women within a radius of several hundred miles, she lives in gut-wrenching poverty.

"Maybe I can start an egg business like my friend Chatri," Tanika begins with a shy smile.

"You can't start there," Sankul explains. "It takes three or four loans to work your way up to such a large investment. We have to think smaller."

Tanika nods with new understanding, then pivots, "My cousin Mitali has done well with the minivan she rents."

Once again Sankul sets her friend straight. "That requires an even larger investment. It has taken your cousin over five years to work her way up to a vehicle. We're beginners and have to start much smaller."

"How about puffed rice," another woman suggests helpfully. "It takes very little money, and I've heard that many women in nearby villages are now doing well with this."

"That's the problem," Damini says. "Too many people are in that business, and profits could drop."

For a moment, Tanika considers quitting the group. But her determination to persevere hardens when images from recent weeks flood through her mind. Three months earlier when her husband sold his rice crop for far less than he had expected, he had taken it out on her. He came home one evening screaming obscenities, assaulted her, accused her of dragging him into poverty, called her ugly, and threw her and their three daughters into the street.

Under normal circumstances in her village, a divorce such as this would have been a death sentence for Tanika and her children. But these weren't normal circumstances. One day as Tanika sat worrying about her family's next meal, her neighbor Sankul told her about a group of people from the city who would loan money to women like her as a means of helping them start new businesses. She felt an intoxicating rush of hope after her first information meeting. But soon her familiar feelings of dread and shame returned. It was only Sankul's frequent reminders of what her future would likely be without the loan that kept her from giving up.

After a quiet moment, Tanika tries again, "You all know that I have earned money in the past by collecting hair from the local barbershops and making wigs."

"Yes, and they're beautiful," Sankul responds. "But you haven't been able to live off of that." As a gentle but unrelenting rain starts to beat its tattoo on the tin roof over the five women, Tanika continues to articulate her partially formed idea.

"You're right; I can't count on wig making. But I know of a place that will buy hair and use the oil from the hair follicles to make health products. I was thinking that if I could find new ways to gather hair,

I could sell it to that company and make enough money to feed my family."

"How do you propose to do that?" asked Payal, the shiest of the five would-be entrepreneurs.

"I'll gladly give you the hair from my hairbrushes. It does me no good," said Damini, offering her support.

"So will I," Kamara chimed in. "And we could get our neighbors to do the same."

Tanika brightens a little. She feels emboldened enough to offer her craziest idea: "I was thinking that maybe I could hire people to gather hair from surrounding neighborhoods," she explained.

"Yes," Sankul agreed, "but how would you pay them?"

"Hire children," Kamara proposed. "You wouldn't have to pay them much, and surely children can gather hair."

"Toys!" Damini shouted. "Buy a batch of small plastic toys and offer them to any child who brings you hair. That way you'll get hair for almost nothing, and the money from your sales will be nearly all profit."

And with that final addition to her original idea, Tanika had all the elements of a business plan. Tanika secured a loan of the equivalent of $20 USD and immediately bought a bag full of inexpensive plastic toys. Then, much like an entrepreneurial Santa Claus, Tanika trudged with her sack of trinkets from village to village.

"I'll let you pick any toy you'd like from the bag if you'll bring me all the hair in your mother and sisters' hairbrushes," Tanika explained to the first group of kids she encountered.

When the word got out that hair earned toys, our unlikely entrepreneur was inundated. Eventually, Tanika sold the hair, repaid her loan, and had capital left over to expand.

A year has passed, and Tanika now has hundreds of women working for her. They gather hair in the villages using toys and sell the hair to Tanika, who then sells it again for a profit. She is a strong, independent single mother who no longer worries about her family's next meal.

## Providing the Influence for Grassroots Entrepreneurship

Why was Tanika able to succeed even though hundreds of millions of people just like her have failed to fight their way out of poverty? Meet Muhammad Yunus, a Nobel laureate whose leadership opened the door for Tanika's entrepreneurial brilliance.

After completing his doctorate in economics in the United States in 1972, Yunus decided to return to his homeland of Bangladesh to become a university professor. As he assumed his comfortable teaching position, he was horrified to discover that just outside the academic compound, hundreds of thousands of people were dying of starvation.

Muhammad Yunus concluded that poverty is sometimes better solved by enabling new behavior than by offering charity.

Everywhere he looked he saw people who worked hard but who were still unable to earn a decent wage. In an attempt to find solutions he interviewed 42 people from a neighboring village. One after another reported that the primary barrier they faced to emerging from poverty was a lack of access to capital.

Few in these villages had traditional jobs because jobs were simply not available. Most, therefore, were self-employed. If they weren't supported by their own small plot of land, they were the proprietor of a tiny craft or service business.

To purchase their inventory or supplies, they needed capital. Usually, it was just a few pennies. Since none had even this small amount, they were forced to turn to local loan sharks who charged over 1,000 percent interest. The interest rate was set at just the point to guarantee that each entrepreneur would exhaust their income repaying the loan and forever be locked in a cycle of debt.

For example, Yunus was dumbfounded when he discovered that a woman who made beautiful handcrafted stools was held in poverty because she lacked the 5 cents she would need to buy supplies each day. Five cents!

Yunus concluded that if he could help villagers access credit at reasonable rates and develop habits of successful repayment, he could improve the financial fortunes of these workers. In total, the 42 people he interviewed needed a paltry $27 to finance their businesses.

Yunus turned to local banks and suggested that they offer loans to these 42 laborers at market rates. There were no takers. In fact, bank executives laughed him out of their offices. As far as they were concerned, if there was no collateral, there would be no loans!

"Usually when my head touches the pillow, I fall asleep within seconds," Yunus told us years later, "But that night I lay in bed ashamed that I was part of a society which could not provide $27 to forty-two able-bodied, hardworking, skilled persons to make a living for themselves."

Dr. Yunus founded what today is a multibillion-dollar banking and business conglomerate known as Grameen Bank, which started a revolution that has given hundreds of millions like Tanika across the world a tool to improve their prospects. The microcredit group that loaned Tanika the starting cash she needed in neighboring India was formed as a direct result of Dr. Yunus's work.

What makes this story even more remarkable is that Dr. Yunus's methods helped not only Tanika but also her four friends who opened small businesses and succeeded—as do 39 out of every 40 people that Dr. Yunus helps. That's correct—98 percent of the people to whom Grameen loans money repay their loans in full—with interest!

But to focus too much on access to capital is to miss part of the brilliance of Yunus's influence plan. Yunus understood that simply borrowing and repaying money would not transform a person's life. Rather, Tanika would have to develop a whole new set of habits to help her transcend her squalid reality. She would need to learn to speak, think, and plan in ways starkly different from her past. And she was less likely to make this dramatic transformation on her own. So Yunus gave her more than a loan—he gave her a team.

Dr. Yunus didn't merely ask Tanika to submit a business plan that *he* would review. He required her first to find four friends, each of whom would submit a plan of her own. Each person from the group would eventually be granted a loan. And with the granting of a loan, each of the other four people would cosign for the debt! That meant that Tanika had to convince her four friends that her business idea would work. She would have to work with them to create a plan that they would first coinvent and then support.

What do you suppose happens when people who have never worked a job and who are currently struggling to afford the basics are being asked to cosign their new teammate's note in case the business fails? They give the most committed kind of help possible. They create smart and workable plans blessed by the full resources of a motivated group.

## HELP HELPS

In Chapter 5, we learned that others influence our motivation in profound ways. Now we add the second of the two social sources of influence: *social ability*. As the Beatles suggested, we're more likely to take on new behaviors when we have "a little help from our friends." These friends provide us with access to their brains, give us the strength of their hands, and even allow us to make use of resources we'd lack without them. Those around us form the "social capital" of our lives—the human resources that help us surpass our individual limits.

We're often blind to the degree to which we depend upon the enabling influence of others. Even the modest individual business savvy of Tanika's five colleagues, when combined with the deep awareness they had of local market realities, enabled her to invent a viable business concept. And the social permission they gave her to step into a more empowered view of herself enabled her to exceed the limitations of her culture.

We often overlook the need to provide *social ability* to those we try to lead because we fail to appreciate the social complexity of human behavior. Take eating, for example—a behavior it would be easy to conclude is mediated largely by individual preferences and desires. But it isn't. Researchers from Cornell University found, for example, that if you dine with one other person, you'll eat 25 percent more than if you eat alone. And if you eat with four or more others, you'll eat over 60 percent more than if you eat alone![1]

These dramatic differences become obvious when you notice how many socially enabling behaviors happen in the course of a typical group lunch. For example, the very fact that five people are eating means the lunch will take longer. And the longer you eat, the more you eat. When a fellow diner passes a bread basket around the table, others are far more likely to select a piece and place it on their plate. If one person orders a dish that is higher in fat or calories than you'd typically order, you're more likely to consider it. Coffee? Dessert? I will if you are. And heaven forbid, the group agrees to split the bill rather than ask for separate checks! When this happens, research shows that each person tends to buy (and eat) more.[2]

Closer to the workplace, let's say you'd like to influence your team toward more spirited dialogue and intellectual honesty. You hope that more vigorous engagement will lead to better decisions and more unified action. You're unlikely to succeed unless you're willing to play a pivotal enabling role.

For example, when the senior leader in a team meeting resists weighing in on deliberations until others have fully expressed varying points of view, greater candor results. Likewise, if the boss is willing to play devil's advocate—openly acknowledging weaknesses in their own position—others are more likely to join the conversation. Because vital behaviors are enacted by individuals and sometimes even done in private, it's easy to miss the crucial facilitating or debilitating role others play.

Like Yunus, effective leaders anticipate the many ways people might need social support as they practice new behaviors. They find ways to provide:

- Permission
- Modeling
- Help
- Coaching

We will explore each of these in the following sections.

## PROVIDE PERMISSION

Source 4, social ability, is tough to tease apart from source 3, social motivation. Anytime you provide assistance to someone, you're simultaneously providing encouragement. You're in essence saying, "I want you to do this." For example, the very fact that Tanika's group members are helping her brainstorm a business strategy gives her social permission to take a larger place in society than her oppressive marriage and upbringing had previously offered.

But there are times when your leadership must include even more formal permission if you want people to exceed past social norms. Success might depend on engaging formal leaders in helping others break unwritten rules that would otherwise constrain their behavior.

Meet Jess. At this very moment he's sweating like an Olympic boxer. That's because he's about to tell a lie, and he's afraid he'll get caught. As Jess starts to speak, his panic makes his throat constrict to the size of a straw. After faking a coughing seizure, Jess eventually squeaks out the big, fat lie that's sure to get him in trouble.

"No problem," Jess mutters. "We're right on target."

Jess isn't the only fibber at the table. Everyone in this product development meeting is stretching the truth. In fact, at the 1,500-person software development group where Jess works, lying about readiness is so common that Jess and his colleagues have given it a special name. It's called playing "project chicken."

Here's how the game is played. You say you're ready with your part of a project when you aren't, in the hope that someone else will admit that he or she will need to extend the deadline. The first person to lose nerve and say, "I need more time" is the chicken. And like the vehicular version of the same game, once someone swerves, everyone else is safe. All the others are off the hook because they'll benefit from the new extended deadline, only they didn't have to admit they messed up.

In this particular meeting, most of the team leaders at the table, just like Jess, are dangerously behind. Yet none of them will admit it. This time, nobody swerves, the deadline isn't extended, and as a result of their combined lying, a major product release will soon end in disaster. When we first started working with this company, it was on the brink of bankruptcy. It had not met a product release date in years. And when the company finally did release products, those products typically cost twice as much as they should have. Morale was at an all-time low, so the company was losing far too many of its most talented players.

Mike, the newly appointed VP of development, was tasked with turning this situation around. He had already identified the vital behavior he had to influence. He knew that if he could find a way to both motivate and enable employees up and down the organization to speak up early and honestly about problems, the company would improve morale, reduce costs, and gain control of the schedule.

When we first met Mike, he had already tried several strategies. He had offered training, he had identified opinion leaders and asked them to help influence change, and he had even created an anonymous survey to measure whether or not behavior was changing. Still, few were stepping forward. Over time, Mike began to realize that Jess and his colleagues were not isolated actors. Lying in order to look good had been reinforced by managers, directors, and vice presidents. It was more than a habit; it was a norm. And few were changing because few felt they had true permission to break it.

So Mike looked for a way to get the very managers whose disapproval employees feared to empower people to share bad news. In a senior staff meeting he charged every one of his top leaders with teaching the communication classes that had formerly been taught by professional trainers. He knew that in a case like this *who* teaches is as important as *what* is taught.

Every two weeks the manager who had previously sent subtle signals about suppressing candor taught a two-hour session on how to speak up about project risks.

In the first two sessions Jess listened passively and cynically. By the third session he began to consider that his manager's encouragement might be sincere—so he gave it a shot. He gently raised a risk to a customer commitment. In the thrall of his training role, his boss responded in textbook form, acknowledging Jess's integrity and giving due consideration to the new information.

By the sixth session many of Jess's peers had begun to open up. Within a matter of months powerful new norms emerged, and Mike's vital behavior of candor under pressure flourished. Within a year the organization launched two product releases on time and on budget, and morale was at an all-time high.

When old habits are sustained by formal leaders, formal leaders need to be part of the solution. Engaging them in teaching roles can be an effective way of ensuring that people are not just encouraged (source 3) but enabled (source 4) to adopt new behavior. When leaders teach, they implicitly extend formal permission to enable others to behave in new ways.

## PROVIDE MODELING

Sometimes people need an example of what a new behavior could look like in the real world. People need to see people like them putting the behavior into practice in a way they find credible.

One of the sacrosanct rules at The Other Side Academy is to tell the truth. Older students tell newer ones that "You stop growing when you start lying." When you lie you disconnect from authentic connection to the rest of the house. And connection is your only hope of learning to live differently in a healthy community.

In spite of all these admonitions, one student, Kade, lied. In his initial interview he was asked whether he had any history with others in the house. He chose to withhold the fact that he had both romantic and criminal connections to three other students. For whatever reason, he decided the safest path was to fib. He had been doing it his whole life, so he saw no reason that this moment should be any different.

But six months into his tenure, Kade started to feel differently. One day he saw one of his closest peers in a yellow shirt. A yellow shirt means students are on "contract." A contract is a form of discipline for those who have committed very serious offenses—offenses that violate the trust of the community. Those on contract work longer hours as a way of demonstrating their desire to regain others' trust.

Kade approached his friend and asked, "Why are you on contract?"

"I lied in my initial interview," his friend responded. "I'm sick of being dirty in my life. I came here to do something different. So I admitted what I did, and now I have a two-week contract."

Kade couldn't sleep that night. The next morning Kade, a thief, a drug dealer, a junkie, and a liar, decided it was time to become an honest man. He wore a yellow shirt and endured extra work hours for a month with pride as he showed his commitment to change.

Kade had carried his secret for months and had intended to carry it forever, until a persuasive model convinced him to make an enormous sacrifice to regain his integrity.

## How Modeling Solved a Corporate Crisis

One of the most important reasons to involve opinion leaders (see Chapter 5) in your influence efforts is that they make the most credible models. For example, after careful deliberation, Carol Bernick, former president of Alberto Culver, a beauty supply company, concluded that saving the struggling company would require more than a few new bestselling products. Rather, she needed to engage thousands of employees in questioning and improving every aspect of the enterprise.

A key to the legendary turnaround of Alberto Culver (before its acquisition by Unilever) was the pivotal role of 70 carefully identified opinion leaders from across the enterprise. Bernick spent generous amounts of time with them over months, listening to their concerns, soliciting their ideas, and earning their trust. Then she invited any who were willing to take on the role of growth development leader (GDL) and tasked them with enabling greater engagement from employees with whom they had natural influence.

For example, GDLs were often encouraged to bring a colleague of their choosing to privileged sessions with Bernick. There they'd witness candid exchanges between GDLs and their president, which taught them patterns for participation that they carried back to their teams.[3]

## Saving Lives with Peer Help

Influential models have been the key to saving lives in Hope Squad, a peer-to-peer suicide prevention program. Greg Hudnall, a former public school principal, dedicated his life to saving lives after losing some of his students to suicide. The breaking point came when a fourth grader at a local elementary school committed suicide—at a park next to the school. The day of the tragedy was endless. At 1:30 a.m., after agonizing hours with police, students, teachers, and the grief-stricken family, Dr. Hudnall returned to his car and sobbed inconsolably until a resolve settled in his soul that has guided his life ever since: "I will do everything I can to prevent any other child from taking their life."[4]

Years later, there are Hope Squads in 1,600+ schools across 43 US states, Canada, and other countries. One of the drivers behind how these squads work is that parents and teachers are sometimes the last to know when a child is at risk. Thus, change must engage kids themselves. Dr. Hudnall's first goal was to foster a vital behavior where peer students practiced QPR:

- *Question* (open a conversation when you see signals of concern),
- *Persuade* (urge those at risk to get help), and
- *Refer* (proactively connect them with resources).

Hope Squads fight student suicide by engaging student opinion leaders.

To get this model to work, Hudnall first identified opinion leaders. He asked students across the school for the names of those they'd turn to if they needed help or a listening ear. Those who were identified most frequently by peers were invited to participate in the Hope Squad and receive special training.

Today a lifesaving army of 45,000 student leaders are charged with modeling suicide prevention habits for other students. For example, one Hope Squad student noticed that another student was having a tough day. He didn't even know the boy, but he could tell something was off. He called the boy after school and invited him to the mall with him and some friends so he could create an opportunity to question him a bit. After some initial hesitation, the boy admitted he had gone home and loaded his father's gun, preparing to use it on himself. While they were at the mall, the boy's father returned home, discovered the loaded gun sitting on a table, and intervened to get his son needed help. The boy is alive and doing well today.

The remarkable influence of these peer models of caring intervention has resulted in thousands of kids getting timely help, including many who benefited from hospital admission prior to carrying out plans for self-harm.

In most communities, culture changes only as fast as opinion leaders model new behaviors.

## PROVIDE HELP

Sometimes people need more than a model or simple permission—they need specific help. It might be a tool, some resource, the right information, or even a hand.

We travel next to South Africa to study the work of Garth Japhet. Dr. Japhet began his career as a medical doctor, then wound a circuitous path to spend 16 years as the CEO of Soul City, a South African nonprofit working to stop violence against women. In South Africa, as in far too much of the world, violence against women is endemic. One in nine women will be raped at least once in her lifetime. One in five will be physically or emotionally abused by her partner.

One of Dr. Japhet's most crucial insights was that such violence is systemic. It isn't simply about an out-of-control domestic partner making isolated decisions in the privacy of a home. It is a habit that is socially sustained by legal authorities, parents, peers, neighbors, clergy, and scores of others. The behavior is modeled, enabled, taught, and reinforced in profound ways. Therefore, changing it required immense social intervention as well. If *everyone* is sustaining the problem, *everyone* will likewise be required to enable change.

Japhet also understood that many in South African society disapproved of the abuse—both women and men. And yet these people felt unable to exert sufficient influence to change the behavior they despised. For example, Japhet suspected there were thousands of moments when neighbors would witness or overhear awful episodes of abuse, but felt paralyzed in inaction for lack of a safe and effective way of intervening. So Japhet transformed a common household item into a tool for social change. In his own words:

> *On the TV program Soul City, we purposely created a well-respected teacher, Thabang, who repeatedly abused his likable wife, Matlakala. Viewers—both male and female—quickly concluded that Matlakala didn't deserve the abuse as tradition had often indicated. She was pleasant, easy to get along with, and nothing more than an innocent victim. Equally curious, Thabang was mostly a reasonable and good person—much like themselves.*

In one episode neighbors hear Thabang beating poor Matlakala, and they can take it no longer, so they decide to let Thabang know that his actions aren't going unobserved. But how could they let Thabang know without being too intrusive? How could they do it without putting themselves at physical risk?

In the crucial episode, neighbors gather outside Thabang's front door and bang pots and pans. They don't say a word; they just bang pots and pans. Thabang becomes embarrassed and runs from his own house. In future episodes, we see his reluctance to face a repeat of the humiliating night. Instead, he looks for better outlets for his feelings of impotence and rage.

Garth Japhet created a novel way neighbors could help spouses in the act of being abused.

Following this episode, people in townships across South Africa, upon hearing the sounds of spousal abuse next door, began to stand in front of their neighbors' homes and bang pots and pans. What they had lacked was not motivation to intervene, they needed the ability. They needed a tool. Sensing that, Japhet avoided piling on more lectures and instead offered a tool. He enabled them to practice a new behavior.

## Act Like an Influencer

When Rich Sheridan of Menlo Software decided to redesign how his employees create software (from top to bottom), he wanted to make sure that individuals didn't feel alone, isolated, or cut off—or like the sole possessors of certain knowledge, which would make them indispensable and unable to take vacations. So Rich put code writers in teams of two—sharing one computer.

At first, this cramped everyone's style. Everyone wanted to sit in the driver's seat and write their own code. Soon the teams found that with one person typing and one co-designing and watching, they caught errors early on—cutting their time on fixing errors (something everyone hates) from 40 percent of their working time to no time at all. They also reduced "knowledge silos," situations in which only one person knew what was going on.

Now there were two or more experts working on every job. "Since then, we've never had to turn down a vacation request," Rich explains. By creating interdependent pairs (meaning everyone has someone to lean on), just about every measure has improved—including morale.

At Spectrum Healthcare, the provision of help came in the form of Purple People. The day doctors and nurses were instructed to begin using a new electronic medical records system, many felt anxious. The new initiative would fail if harried doctors who were not direct employees of Spectrum Healthcare hospitals elected to use sticky notes and scratch pads rather than stepping up to the keyboard.

Once again, wise leaders refused to simply pile on more reasons for complying (You'll save lives! You'll save time!). Instead, they trained opinion leaders from throughout the organization to give support for the most common struggles. During the first week the new system was implemented, these opinion leaders all wore purple T-shirts emblazoned with the title "Purple People." Employees and doctors were instructed to find a purple person at the first sign of trouble. The release went flawlessly, with 98 percent compliance within 48 hours.

Among all the leaders we have studied, those who faced the biggest risks also worked the hardest to provide assistance to influence change during crucial moments.

All of us have behaviors we struggle to change, then relapse into past practices. Arranging for help from others is not a sign of weakness, but an admission of reality. We often can't do it alone.

## PROVIDE COACHING

Shakespeare once said, "For the eye sees not itself / But by reflection, by some other things." Sometimes as people struggle to adopt new behaviors, the first assistance they need is a more accurate view of themselves. Next, they need help figuring out how to properly practice new and better habits. In other words, they need coaching.

We once worked with Lauren, an aspiring executive who had been told she needed to "lean in" more at work. Her boss told her that she was brilliant but invisible. She took the challenge and began speaking up more in meetings and volunteering occasionally to present ideas. And the more she leaned in, the more her credibility plummeted. She wasn't a very persuasive or effective public speaker. To put it bluntly, she had an uncanny ability to whip a crowd into a nap.

This all changed with two pieces of advice from an insightful friend. Lauren knew what she wanted, but she didn't know what it looked like. So she enlisted a coworker to give her some coaching. After watching her carefully in multiple settings, her colleague told her, "Pick up the speed by 10 percent. And always start with your conclusion."

It was hard to hear the truth about how she came across (slow and disorganized). But the instant Lauren put the coaching into practice, she could read the difference in the alertness and engagement of her audiences. Her influence increased and her comfort in social settings soared.

What Lauren needed to change was not more motivation; she needed a coach.

## Act Like an Influencer

David Levin and his colleagues at KIPP schools don't just want to help their 125,000 at-risk children get to college. They want to influence them in such a way that they graduate—opening otherwise unimaginable futures. For years KIPP's 33 percent college graduation rate appeared to be a marvel when compared with an 8.3 percent likelihood for similar kids who didn't go to a KIPP school. Then Levin's team replaced expert school counselors with what they call "Near Peers." Near Peers are former KIPP-sters freshly graduated from college. KIPP offers them the chance to work for a maximum of two years helping kids a few years behind them traverse the hazards of early college life. The shift from experts to opinion leaders has produced remarkable improvements—with 45 percent of KIPP alumni who graduate from high school now completing a four-year degree. Near Peers don't just give encouragement, they give hard-earned advice for dealing with breakups, stretching food dollars, and choosing classes.

## Coaching in Thailand

One influential leader is credited with saving over five million lives, in part because of his wisdom in providing real-time coaches. When Dr.

Wiwat Rojanapithayakorn came on the scene in the Ratchaburi province of Thailand in the early 1980s, the AIDS epidemic was raging out of control. As a middle manager in the health ministry at the time, he recognized that if things didn't change, the death rate in Thailand would soon eclipse that of anywhere else in the world.

He also realized that given there were no vaccines or even effective treatments at the time, the only hope of saving lives was to treat the crisis as a social science problem, not a medical science one. In other words, by influencing behavior.

Dr. Wiwat went to work using every principle we've outlined so far. First, he ensured that the goal was clear: *Halt the spread of AIDS.*

He worked hard to establish credible measures of infections and deaths across his province. Next, he studied the vital behaviors that would be key to saving lives. It was soon clear that the primary path of new infections nationwide was the sex trade.

In a country where the majority of Thai men were at least occasional clients of the sex trade, the virus that causes AIDS was not confined to subgroups like IV drug users sharing needles or single people with multiple sex partners. Instead, it was following husbands and life partners back to many homes and families in the country.

Through rigorous study, Dr. Wiwat zeroed in on a crucial moment that held the key to success. A typical scenario looks like this: Achara, a tragically young woman, is exploited to offer sex services by the owner of a go-go bar in a seedy area of town. A foreign tourist takes an interest in Achara and negotiates for her services. In passing, during the price discussion, she mentions that he will be required to use a condom. He flushes red and demands that she back down. She makes a nervous attempt to hold her ground. At this point, she realizes the brothel owner is following the conversation. He tersely shakes his head at her. Achara begins to relent. The tourist offers a substantial tip. Achara has a life-or-death decision to make.

Dr. Wiwat realized that success meant finding a way to influence the outcome of hundreds of thousands of moments just like this one in thousands of dark corners of Thailand every single day. If he failed, young women like Achara, and the many who contracted the virus through them, would continue to die.

As part of Wiwat's influence plan, he got Achara and other workers the coaching and the authority they would need to practice the vital behavior. "Women in these circumstances," he told us, "are at an overwhelming power disadvantage. If we don't address that, they can't protect themselves."

So Wiwat invited brothel owners to attend a meeting in a hotel ballroom. Many were nervous at first about attending such a public gathering. He ensured they were properly motivated to show up by explaining that their choice was to either attend or be shut down by the police for 30 days. They all showed up.

The meeting agenda was simple, brief, and straightforward. Neither condoning nor condemning their work, he simply urged them to show greater concern for the health and well-being of their workers by complying with 100 percent condom use from today forward. He reasoned that demanding safety would not cause a loss of customers to competitors if all held firm on the same requirements. All nodded obediently.

Wiwat then added that "mystery shoppers" from the health ministry would be routinely visiting their establishments and attempting to secure services without condom use. Should any employee fail to demand condom use, the brothel would be shut down for 30 days. The nodding seemed more vigorous. Wiwat's hope was that this intervention would motivate owners to give sex workers the authority to decline unprotected sex services.

He next set to work on solving an even more difficult problem—empowering teenage girls to hold boundaries with sexually aroused and inebriated customers—often customers who would take offense at being told no by a woman. Step one was to engage former sex workers who knew how to handle these moments to teach workshops to younger girls. The workshop leaders identified those within each brothel who were more skillful at resisting pressure. They enlisted their commitment to provide coaching and backup to less confident workers when the pressure was on. Participants engaged in deliberate practice of these confrontations with the very coworkers who would be around them when the going got tough. Furthermore, they knew who they could turn to in a crisis if they needed help.

The results were striking. Within days condom use became the norm, increasing from 14 percent before the intervention to 90 percent immediately following. And as expected, the number of new AIDS infections declined precipitously—ultimately decreasing by 88 percent within a couple of years.

While it's impossible to determine the names of those whose lives were saved, we know that an entire nation was blessed by a leader who understood the intricacies of influence.

## THE POWER OF SOCIAL CONNECTIONS

The difference between success and failure in health, career, business, and life often comes down to the enabling role of others. Patterns of poverty or prosperity, for example, are not just about individual capability. They are enabled or inhibited by the kind of mentoring, guidance, and connections an individual is given early on.

Look at the profusion of online communities these days to provide mental health counseling, life coaching, addiction recovery support, knitting advice, and even culinary insect preparation. Tom Boyle of British Telecom coined the expression *network quotient* (NQ) to highlight the importance of a person's ability to form connections with others. He argues that from a career standpoint a person's NQ is now more important than their intelligence quotient (IQ).

The behaviors we form depend upon the people around us. The most effective leaders ensure that social enabling is built into every attempt to influence positive change.

## SUMMARY: SOCIAL ABILITY

Bad behavior is often sustained by a complex network of other people—those who model, coach, and demand compliance with old norms. Effective leaders recognize this and take steps to ensure those they want to influence have the social support they need to break free of old constraints. Specifically, they build plans to provide:

1. **Social permission.** Those with formal or informal authority must overtly enable behavior that might have been taboo in the past.
2. **Modeling.** If a picture is worth a thousand words, a live model who shows what vital behaviors look like in action is worth millions.
3. **Help.** Help is needed when people haven't yet mastered the new behavior.
4. **Real-time coaching to lift others to the next level.** Learning is accelerated when coaching immediately follows an initial attempt at new behavior.

Influential leaders understand that social ability is crucial to any effort to make change inevitable.

We depend on assistance from those around us when attempting to form new behaviors. The most effective leaders make sure to grant permission, model the correct behaviors, extend help when needed, and provide real-time coaching to those they are leading.

|  | MOTIVATION | ABILITY |
|---|---|---|
| **PERSONAL** | Help Them Love What They Hate | Help Them Do What They Can't |
| **SOCIAL** | Provide Encouragement | Provide Assistance |
| **STRUCTURAL** | **Reward with Care** | Change the Environment |

# 7

# REWARD WITH CARE

## *Source 5: Structural Motivation*

---

*Even small rewards can help people make remarkable change.*

---

So far, we've explored both personal and social influence. Now we step away from human factors and examine source 5, *structural motivation*: how to optimize the power of *things* such as rewards, perks, bonuses, salaries, and the occasional boot in the rear. Most leaders need no convincing to align rewards with vital behaviors. They fully believe that incentives change behavior. So our advice here may surprise you.

Your goal with structural motivation should not be to overwhelm people to change. Rather, it should be primarily to remove *dis*incentives—to "change the economy" as it were.

Most leaders run the risk of relying too much on incentives. But if bad behavior is deeply entrenched, odds are that the current system is positively encouraging the exact behaviors you don't want. Changing the economy means ensuring that positive and negative incentives aren't undermining the influence message you're trying to send. But the real work of motivating change shouldn't be done with incentives. Sources 1 (personal motivation) and 3 (social motivation) should do the heavy lifting.

## USE EXTRINSIC REWARDS THIRD

Stories of well-intended rewards that inadvertently backfire are legion. One hospital, for example, found that anesthesiologists who were paid based only on the work they did with their own patients were less willing to jump in and help one another when someone else's patient was reacting badly.

Consider some attempts by the former Soviet Union to dabble in incentive schemes. In the energy sector, rubles were being thrown away in the search for oil reserves because Soviet workers received bonuses according to the number of feet they drilled. It turns out that it's far easier to drill many shallow holes than to drill a few deeper ones. Instead of following the geological advisories to drill deep to find existing reserves, workers were happy merely poking the surface over and over—turning up very little oil. After all, it's what they were rewarded for doing.[1]

An executive we know decided that her employees weren't as innovative as they needed to be, so she instituted a simple suggestion program. Employees were encouraged to find ways to bring in more revenue or reduce costs—with the promise of bonuses and prizes for validated contributions. Employees were *less* rather than *more* inclined to offer improvement ideas with the bonus attached. Previously they'd occasionally offer ideas out of the simple desire to improve work life. But now, the only proposals they put time into developing were those that might get them a substantial payout. The net effect was less improvement and more negotiation over who got paid what for the big ideas.

The primary cause of most of these debacles is that individuals attempt to influence change by using rewards as their *first* motivational strategy. When it comes to *motivating* change, effective leaders use rewards *third*. They first ensure that vital behaviors are given the proper moral frame. The best reason for people to adopt new behaviors is because they feel right, good, or meaningful. They're *personally motivating*.

Next, they line up social support. They ensure that formal and informal leaders are doing their best to turn the new behaviors into new social norms. Only then do they examine the influence of structured rewards or sanctions.

When people aren't doing the right things for the right reasons, piling on "carrots and sticks" is more likely to create unintended consequences.

For example, in a classic experiment from 1973, Dr. Mark Lepper[2] found that kids who were rewarded for doing something they already enjoyed began to enjoy the activity less. Researchers watched small children playing with toys in a nursery to determine which toy they preferred. They next told them they would be given a favorite snack each time they played with that toy. No surprise, the kids played with the toy more. At least while the snacks were in play. When the reward was removed, kids played with their previously favorite toy *much less*!

Dr. Lepper revealed that rewarding people for engaging in an activity that is already satisfying may work against you. Think of the implications. You want your daughter to learn to love reading with the same joy you have. You notice that she's starting to pick up the behavior on her own, so you decide to reinforce it. To encourage her, you create an incentive program. Every time she picks out a book on her own and reads it, you give her $5. She loves the plan and starts reading more, and she spends her earnings on a new video game. It's not long until she's able to buy several games.

After a while, you think that you've rewarded reading enough and that it has become its own reward. So you drop the incentive. Surely your encouragement has helped your daughter learn to love reading good books even more.

But your plan backfires. The minute you stop paying your daughter for reading, she turns to her games and reads less than she did before you offered incentives. Apparently she has learned to earn money to purchase games, and the incentive you tried didn't leave the impression you wanted. She's just like those nursery school kids.

The explanation for this phenomenon became known as "the overjustification effect." If people already enjoy something, incentives can crowd out the intrinsic pleasure they receive. People begin to attribute their engagement as a response to the incentive rather than the pleasure—like professional athletes whose colossal salary causes them to lose their initial love of the game itself. Once the reward is removed, the person believes that the activity isn't as much fun as he or she judged earlier, so he or she does it less often.

Remember what we learned from source 1, personal motivation: *How you frame is how you feel.* The sources of motivation a leader relies on can influence how others frame the activity. If the leader frames an activity as a moral good or a pleasurable pursuit, they encourage others to connect to deep and sustainable reasons for engaging in the activity. If they frame it as socially desirable, they are similarly likely to engage. But overreliance on incentives can cause people to lose connection with their previous moral and social motivations.

For example, frustrated leaders in an Israeli daycare center attempted to use incentives to foster more conscientious behavior from parents. Parents were expected to pick up their children promptly at 3:30 p.m. when daycare services were scheduled to end. Many would arrive 5, 10, or even 15 minutes late, an inconsiderate inconvenience to the staff. One day the staff announced that going forward, tardy parents would be charged $5 for every 30 minutes they arrived past 3:30 pm. What would you predict happened? And more importantly, why?

What had been a relative handful of outliers suddenly became the norm. Far *more* parents began showing up late. Why? Because leaders had changed the frame. Previously, parents saw their pickup time as a moral (I made a promise to be there at 3:30 p.m.) or a social (I don't want staff to be mad at me) issue. By assigning a price, they inadvertently turned it into an economic calculation ($5 for 30 minutes of high-quality babysitting? You can have little Judith for the whole weekend!).

Using incentives third will serve you well even in moments of spontaneous influence. Think back to our coauthor whose son was detained by police for throwing water balloons at cars. He retrieves his son from the police station and begins the silent ride home. When Dad finally breaks the silence, the first words out of his mouth will reveal the way Dad frames his son's delinquency. If Dad starts with, "You're in big trouble now!" he has framed it economically (source 5). Dad is suggesting that Brian should regret his behavior because it's leading to extrinsic consequences. If he begins with, "You've embarrassed our family!" he has framed it socially (source 3). It's about reputation, respect, and social sanction. Fortunately, in this situation, Dad chose to offer a moral frame: "Imagine you're driving a car and suddenly a big hard object slams into your windshield. Maybe even cracks it. How would that feel?" He encouraged his son to empathize with the driver of the vehicle they targeted (source 1).

This sensitivity was on display in a March 2020 press conference with then-governor Jay Inslee of Washington state. Early in the Covid-19 pandemic, Washington, and many other regions of the world, announced mandatory shelter-in-place and mask policies. As Inslee explained the new policies, a reporter asked Inslee, "What are the penalties for not abiding by the ban?" Inslee could have referred to potential fines or incarceration (source 5). But he didn't. He understood that the only sustainable motivations for change would have to be moral and social. He answered, "The penalties are you might be killing your grand-dad if you don't do it. And I'm serious about this. The principle . . . is for people to understand the consequences of community responsibility."

Jay Inslee resisted the temptation to turn a moral choice into an economic one.

The bottom line is not that incentives don't matter. They do. But if not combined with clear moral and social messaging, they are more likely to cause distracting chaos than positive change.

### Act Like an Influencer

We asked our hospitality expert, Danny Meyer, how he uses incentives to motivate great customer service. "We don't do much with incentives," he concluded. "Well, we pool all tips, but lots of places do that. We believe that creating exceptional customer experiences requires an entire team. So tips are a reflection not just of one person's effort—but the whole team's. However, people don't serve customers just to get tips. They do it because they enjoy it and because they're part of a great culture that promotes it." Danny shows us that the heavy lifting of leadership is done by sources 1 and 3. His goal is to ensure source 5 is simply aligned with the results and behaviors he wants.

## USE INCENTIVES WISELY

Effective leaders do eventually use rewards and punishments. For instance, if you don't repay a loan to Muhammad Yunus's Grameen Bank, your borrower group has to pay it back for you. And remember, they know where you live!

When Dr. Wiwat wanted the attention of brothel owners in his AIDS campaign, he let them know there would be legal consequences if they failed to protect their workers. And if a person in a rural African village calls out her neighbor who is not properly filtering water for Guinea worm larvae, village leaders reward her with an attractive T-shirt (emblazoned with a Guinea worm disease eradication logo).

Incentives help. So, the question is, how do you use them wisely?

First, as we learned, make sure they don't overwhelm other intrinsic and social motivators. Let's look at three other guidelines for implementing incentives effectively:

- Think small.
- Reward behavior, not just results.
- Punish sparingly.

## Think Small

You don't need to go overboard with big gestures and pricey incentives. Even small rewards can help people make remarkable changes. For example, Johns Hopkins Hospital completed a study of alcoholics who had been admitted to the hospital to, of all things, drink alcohol—but only in moderate quantities. The idea of the project was to help those who struggle with alcoholism achieve moderation rather than abstinence.

To influence patients' behavior, each day staff members determined residential privileges on the basis of how much alcohol the patients consumed. If they drank too much, they were given pureed food instead of the normal offering. Their amount of consumption also affected phone privileges, visiting hours, and so on. When compared to control patients who were simply told how much to drink with no incentives, experimental subjects were 60 percent more likely to reach their target consumption level.

If you find it hard to believe that simple incentives can help patients break free from the grip of alcoholism, you'll be amazed to find they help with something as addictive as cocaine. Dr. Stephen Higgins, professor of psychology and psychiatry and director of Vermont Center on Behavior and Health, developed a method of rewards as incentives for outpatient rehab programs.[3] In the programs, participants must submit a urine sample three times a week. Higgins's strategy said that if all three samples tested negative, subjects received a bonus voucher that they could exchange for goods and services provided by the research staff.

Even Higgins was surprised to find that "a stack of vouchers can outweigh the powerful urge to use cocaine."

Obviously, vouchers alone wouldn't be enough to keep cocaine addicts clean. All six sources of influence are required for lasting change. However, when used with other sources of influence, 90 percent of those who were also given incentives finished the 12-week treatment program, whereas only 65 percent of non-voucher subjects completed the program. The long-term effects were similarly impressive.

To show how small incentives can be powerful motivators for almost anyone, take a look at your luggage. If you're like millions of other travelers around the world, you sport a shiny tag displaying your frequent flyer status like it's a Nobel Prize. It's almost embarrassing to acknowledge the way these programs have reshaped our behavior. In the early days of these programs ambitious status-seekers would take useless flights at the end of the year just to ensure they "qualified" for the next higher ranking. Today since you can accumulate points for any purchases, it's not uncommon for people to funnel everything they can think of through their frequent flyer associated credit card to ensure they get points and status. Do we respond to incentives? Yes! In fact, travelers have become so obsessed with maximizing their miles that the dollar value of unused frequent flyer miles on the planet now exceeds all the cash circulating in the US economy.

It's important to add that there is often much more going on with some incentives than their economic value alone. For example, when staff in a cocaine recovery program hand out a voucher, some recipients will experience intrinsic (I accomplished something!) and social motivation (the staff respect me). A frequent flyer luggage tag is about social status signaling (Look everyone, I'm a Titanium Albatross!) as much as a path to free travel. And that's the point. Well-implemented incentives don't need to be big, because they're used as vehicles for all three sources of motivation, not just one.

For example, we saw how a well-packaged brass goose could light a fire in hundreds of highly paid executives. A consulting firm in the United States decided to offer awards for top execs who completed training assignments. The plan was simple. Senior leaders would meet weekly in a world-acclaimed training program where they would be given specific behavioral goals to ensure they practiced what they were learning. The leaders would then report back to their trainer when they had fulfilled their commitment. Each completed assignment earned them points. When they received a threshold number of points, they were publicly presented with a 10-inch-tall brass goose with a retail value of $10.

Leaders read lengthy books, wrote up case studies, filled out forms, and moved heaven and earth to be sure they made it to the trainer by the cutoff time.

It wasn't the cash value of the reward that mattered. It was the symbolic message that motivated behavior. It was the moral and social motivation that gave the token award value.

The Other Side Academy makes impressive use of modest rewards as well. Students quickly learn that with each new accomplishment they receive new privileges. They move from grunt work to increasingly complicated and interesting jobs. As a reward, they get to replace their red freshman shirt with a green sophomore shirt. If they stick with it, they get the blue junior shirt and eventually a coveted black senior shirt. Ultimately students are given $50 per month in "walking-around money" (WAM)—and the privilege of leaving the campus to use it.

These seemingly small incentives are a big deal, and students are as proud of their new shirts as they are of the promotion that came with it.

Shirt colors at The Other Side Academy offer powerful motivation.

We can't resist sharing one more example of modest rewards exerting outsized influence. In a group home for troubled teenage girls, administrators noted an alarming trend. Suicide attempts among residents had increased dramatically. After administrators tried everything from giving emotional speeches, to holding group sessions, to enlisting the help of friends and family—all to no avail—they came up with, of all things, an incentive: If a resident attempted suicide, she would be denied TV privileges for the next week. Suicide attempts dropped to zero.

Without going into the complex psychology of suicide attempts versus suicide gestures and then missing the point of the example, suffice it to say that small incentives that are immediately linked to vital behaviors can yield amazing results with some of the world's most difficult problems. Rewards should be as large as necessary, but no larger, or you risk crowding out the intrinsic (source 1) or social (source 3) motivation they carry with a flashy economic lure (source 5).

---

### Act Like an Influencer

One open-pit mine used simple incentives to boost safe driving practices. The giant trucks used on-site were equipped with GPS systems that measured speed, acceleration, and braking in order to hold drivers accountable for bad behavior. Terrible things had happened in the mine in the past when drivers failed to drive carefully. The new tracking systems gathered data that was combined to create "risky driving scores" for every driver each day. The drivers were grouped into five-person teams. A team's score consisted of whatever the worst score was for a driver on their team.

Teams with the best scores won small weekly prizes—caps, T-shirts, and coffee mugs. These prizes were emblazoned with "Master Driver" logos. Driving safety improved markedly and rapidly following the introduction of this simple way to keep score and reward achievement.

This highly successful incentive system tapped into both personal pride (source 1) and peer pressure (source 3). It used small rewards (source 5) in combination with other sources to promote positive change.

---

### Reward Behavior, Not Just Results

Rewards can be helpful early in a leadership effort when it might be a while before new behavior leads to starkly improved results. In such situations, it's wise to recognize and reward small improvements in behavior along the way.

As simple as this sounds, we're bad at it—especially at work. When polled, employees reveal their number one complaint is that they aren't recognized for their contributions. It seems that people hand out praise as if it were being rationed, usually only for outstanding work. Make a small improvement, and it's highly unlikely that anyone will say or do anything. Each year a new survey publishes the fact that employees would appreciate more praise, and each year we apparently do nothing different.

This is odd in light of the fact that humans are actually quite good at rewarding incremental achievement with their small children. A child makes a sound that approximates "Mama," and members of the immediate family screech in joy, call every single living relative with the breaking news, ask the kid to perform on cue, and then celebrate each new pronouncement with the same enthusiasm you expect they'd display had they trained a newborn to recite "If" by Rudyard Kipling.

However, this ability to see and reward small improvements wanes over time until one day it takes a call from a Nobel Committee to raise an eyebrow. Eventually kids grow up and go to work where apparently the words *good* and *job* aren't allowed to be used in combination, or so suggest employee surveys. There seems to be a permanent divide between researchers and scholars who heartily argue that performance is best enhanced by rewarding incremental improvements, and the rest of the world where people wait for a profound achievement before working up any enthusiasm.

Influential leaders find ways to reward sincere efforts to apply vital behaviors—even when the results are modest. For example, in the groundbreaking book *Kaizen* that inspired a global quality movement, author Masaaki Imai highlights the importance of rewarding effort and not outcome.[4] Imai tells the story of a group of servers whose job it was to serve tea during lunch at one of Matsushita's plants. The servers noted that the employees sat in predictable locations and drank a predictable amount of tea. Rather than put a full container at each place, they calculated the optimum amount of tea to be poured at each table, thus reducing tea leaf consumption by half.

How much did the suggestion save? Only a small sum. Yet the group was given the company's presidential gold medal. Other suggestions saved more money (by an astronomical amount), but this modest proposal captured what the judges thought was the best implementation of vital behaviors. They rewarded the process, knowing that if you reward the actual steps people follow, eventually results take care of themselves.

The behavior you reward will drive the behavior you get. Watch coaches as they speak about the importance of teamwork and then celebrate individual accomplishment. Kids quickly learn that it's the score that counts, not the assist, so they stop playing as a team and play to steal the spotlight instead. Or consider the family who unwittingly enable a loved one's addiction. Their words may say, "You should really stop taking drugs," but their actions say, "As long as you're taking them, we'll give you free rent, use of our cars, and bail whenever you need it." They're rewarding the very behavior they claim to want to change.

For years US politicians wrung their hands over the fact that Americans save so little money. For a time they looked jealously across the ocean at Japanese citizens, who save money at many times the rate of Americans. Some analysts speculated there was just something different about Japanese character. Perhaps they were more willing to sacrifice. But then again, maybe the difference could be attributed in part to incentives. For example, in the United States interest earned on savings is taxable. For many years in Japan it wasn't. In the United States during that same time period, interest on consumer debt, like that from credit cards and home loans, was tax deductible. In Japan it wasn't. Maybe we were more alike than we thought.

So take heed. When behaviors are out of whack, look closely at your rewards. Who knows? Your own incentive system may be causing the problem.

### Act Like an Influencer

A consulting firm asked us to discover why many of its best consultants were leaving. The day we began our work, we were invited to their annual awards luncheon, which happened to be held that same day. The luncheon recognized the "Road Warrior of the Year" with a cash prize. This Road Warrior was the consultant who had spent the most days on the road that year, earning the greatest number of consulting days for the firm.

The winner bounded to the stage, grabbed the oversize check he'd won, and announced he'd use it to buy a high-end Porsche. This reward was plenty motivating, but here was the problem: for four years in a row, these "winners" quit the firm the same year they won the prize—citing work-life balance issues.

The company wanted consultants to stay and grow their careers with them, but they were rewarding behavior that encouraged an unhappy work life.

## Discipline Sparingly

Sometimes you don't have the luxury of rewarding positive performance because the person you'd like to reward never actually does the right thing. In fact, he or she does only the wrong thing—and often. In these cases, if you want to make use of extrinsic reinforcers, you're left with the prospect of disciplining this person. Fortunately, since discipline is from the same family as positive reinforcement, it should have a similar effect. Right?

Maybe not. In hundreds of experiments with laboratory animals and humans, researchers found that punishment decreases the likelihood of a previously reinforced response, but only temporarily. Plus it can produce other undesired effects.

You might gain compliance, but only over the short term. The person in question may actually push back or purposely rebel. And there's a good chance that this person will resent the punishment, thereby putting your relationship at risk.

The goal with discipline is to use only as much as necessary. Some of the most motivating effects of discipline come from anticipation, not the consequence itself. Whenever possible, provide a clear warning to let people know exactly what negative things *will* happen to them if they continue down their current path, but don't actually administer discipline yet. The threat alone may be enough to motivate them to stay clear of the wrong behavior.

### Start with the Suggestion of Discipline

Police in North Carolina provide a potent example of using anticipatory motivation in place of actual punishment.[5] Traditionally, cops tried to put a dent in crime by implementing aggressive search-and-arrest strategies that focused on a targeted area. This blitz strategy tended to provoke public outrage and mobilize a community against the policing efforts, and it rarely created effects that lasted very long. As soon as the cops moved to the next area, new faces came in to fill the old positions, and the bad guys were once again in charge.

With their "Second Chance" strategy, authorities in North Carolina take a different approach. Criminal justice officials invite individuals whom they are about to arrest to attend an offender notification forum. The district attorney's office promises that attendees won't be arrested during a 90-minute meeting where authorities then make use of every source of influence imaginable.

For example, along with the offenders, authorities bring in the attendees' friends, family, and other community opinion leaders who ask the criminals to give up their ways and seek normal employment. Next, public officials clarify existing laws and likely consequences: if you get caught, here's the likely penalty. Following this formal approach, ex-offenders (usually former gang members and drug dealers) talk about what they're currently doing to stay straight. Finally, heads of public agencies explain choices the offenders can make to avoid falling back into their old behaviors, including job programs and what it takes to get signed up.

What makes these Second Chance meetings so effective is not merely that they employ so many sources of influence but also that the meetings do such a persuasive job in making it clear that the offenders *will* be convicted and *will* serve long sentences.

After the first part of the meeting concludes, authorities invite the participants (who might be getting bored with the monologue at this point) to a different room where they see posters tacked to the walls. Under each poster they find a small table with a binder on it. During previous weeks police have gathered evidence, including video footage of each of the attendees making at least one illicit drug sale.

As participants enter the new room, each is told, "Find your poster." When they do, they discover that the poster sports a high-resolution photo of them doing a drug deal. In the adjacent binder, they see all the case evidence the police intend to use to prosecute them. Next the invitees are asked to take a seat and watch a video. At this point the local prosecutor states: "Raise your hand when you see your-self committing a felony." One by one, they do. Next, authorities tell the offenders that they've been put on a special list and will be aggressively prosecuted when caught.

Combine this tactic with support from family and friends as well as job programs, and the results were terrific. Small crimes dropped by 35 percent in certain neighborhoods in North Carolina, and in the three neighborhoods where the initiative was implemented, 24 of 40 alleged dealers have stayed clear of the law.

All this was done without having to haul nearly as many people off to jail in order to catch their attention. Poignant, real, and immediate threats of punishment help keep potential hardened criminals on the straight and narrow.

And to enhance the credibility of their efforts, the authorities never bluff. They invite drug dealers to the open forum, and those who don't come are immediately arrested and prosecuted for the crimes recorded on videotape. Those who go through the program and don't stay with their new job training or do commit a crime are also immediately arrested. Soon the word gets out that the authorities are serious about what they say. Then the mere threat of possible negative consequences becomes much more effective.

## Only Discipline as a Last Resort

The implications here should be clear. There are times when you're simply going to have to discipline someone. A shot across the bow hasn't been enough. You've tried incentives, exerted social pressure, and even appealed to the person's sense of values, but the sources of influence supporting the wrong behavior still remain victorious. It's time to make judicious use of discipline.

This next example may be triggering to some readers. We include it because it illustrates a clear case where discipline is an essential element of influencing desperately needed change. Consider the horrible cases of bride abduction in Ethiopia. Young girls were kidnapped on their way to or from school, raped, and then forced to marry the rapist in an effort to save face. This dreadful practice had survived in silence for generations. Nobody wanted to talk about the issue. However, that changed when a popular radio soap opera addressed the issue head-on. Dr. Negussie Teffera worked with a staff of writers and producers to create an enormously popular radio show titled *Yeken Kignit* ("Looking over One's Daily Life").[6]

Negussie Teffera changed not only attitudes but laws.

In one storyline, a much-admired character on the soap opera, a woman named Wubalem, was abducted and then eventually freed and able to marry the man she really loved. Immediately, this previously taboo topic became part of the public discourse. The popular drama aroused such general indignation that new laws were passed—and, equally important, *enforced*—such that the practice has been largely eradicated in many regions.

Now if a man assaults a young girl, instead of being allowed to keep the victim as his wife, he is put in prison. Notice the influence progression in this case, however. The moral and social case was made first, and the legal punishment last. Real change would not have happened had real punishment not been inflicted. But neither would it have happened had the motivational groundwork for change not been established with sources 1 and 3.

The need for enforcement of standards isn't just a social issue. It's needed at times in a corporate environment as well. One of the first questions we ask employees in companies that complain about a lack of accountability is, "What does it take to get fired around here?" Almost always the answers have nothing to do with poor performance.

"Embarrass the boss" is a common response. Another is a sarcastic "Kill a really valuable coworker." In other words, only raging violations of ethics or political faux pas get the boot. When you hear these types of stories, you can bet that the *lack* of discipline for routine infractions is sending a loud message across the organization.

When the threat of negative consequences isn't enough to influence change, the consequences need to be enforced. Otherwise, you may lose the power of the other sources of influence at play. If you aren't willing to follow through when people violate a core value (such as giving their best effort), that value loses its moral force in the organization.

## SUMMARY: STRUCTURAL MOTIVATION

Administering rewards and discipline can be a tricky business. When you look at the extrinsic motivators you're using to encourage or discourage behavior, take care to adhere to a few helpful principles:

1. **Use extrinsic rewards third.** Get personal and social motivators in place first. Let the value of the behavior itself, along with social influences, carry the bulk of the motivational load.
2. **Use incentives wisely.** Don't be afraid to draw on small, heartfelt tokens of appreciation. Remember, when it comes to extrinsic rewards, less is often more.
3. **Reward behavior, not just results.** Take care to link rewards to the vital behaviors you want to see repeated, not just the results. Sometimes outcomes hide inappropriate behaviors.
4. **Discipline sparingly.** Finally, if you end up having to administer discipline, first take a shot across the bow. Let people know what's coming before you impose the punishment. Then, if all else fails, follow through on the consequences.

|  | MOTIVATION | ABILITY |
|---|---|---|
| **PERSONAL** | Help Them Love What They Hate | Help Them Do What They Can't |
| **SOCIAL** | Provide Encouragement | Provide Assistance |
| **STRUCTURAL** | Reward with Care | **Change the Environment** |

# 8

# CHANGE THE ENVIRONMENT

## *Source 6: Structural Ability*

---

*One of the simplest ways to increase your influence*
*is to make physical and virtual changes that make*
*bad behavior harder and good behavior easier.*

---

We'll now explore one of the most consequential but overlooked sources of influence, which is source 6, *structural ability*: the influence of our physical and virtual environments. We are often blind to the formidable force of the *things* and *information* we're immersed in. And because of that, we often grossly underutilize this relentless source of influence.

One of the best ways to increase people's *ability* to change is to simply modify some aspect of their environment to make the old behavior harder or the good behavior easier.

Let's start with a classic example of influence theory. In the late 1940s, representatives from the National Restaurant Association (NRA) asked William Foote Whyte, a professor at the University of Chicago, to help them with a growing problem.[1] After World War II, Americans began eating out in unprecedented numbers. Unfortunately, the restaurant industry wasn't ready for the surge of customers.

As dining volumes increased, hot conflict grew between waitstaff (typically female) and kitchen crews (typically male). A waitress would rush to the counter, shout an order to busy cooks, then rush back to her customers. If the order was not ready when she returned, she would urge the cook to hurry, shouting expressions of encouragement such as, "Hey, hairball, where's the breaded veal? You got a broken arm or what?"

The cooks usually responded In kind. Later, when the waitress received an incorrect order, the two would exchange still more unflattering remarks. After being yelled at a couple of times, the cooks often took revenge by slowing down. Dr. Whyte even observed cooks turning their backs on the servers and intentionally ignoring them until they left, sometimes in tears.

If you wanted to improve waitstaff relationships with cooks, what would you do? Improve communication skills (source 2)? Create incentives for quality improvement (source 5)? Or perhaps ask more polite staff to mentor their feistier peers (source 3)?

Dr. Whyte recommended that the restaurants use a 50-cent metal spindle to gather orders. He then asked servers to skewer a detailed written order on the spindle. Cooks were then to pull orders off and fill them in whatever sequence seemed most efficient (though generally following a first-in, first-out policy).

Whyte tried the idea at a restaurant the next day. Training consisted of a 10-minute instruction session for both cooks and servers. Managers reported an immediate decrease in conflict and customer complaints. All preferred the new structure, and both groups reported that they were being treated better. The concept spread across the entire industry, resulting in dramatic changes in server/cook relation-ships as well as customer experience.

Sometimes introducing a simple technology or tweaking a process is the fastest path to change.

## FISH DISCOVER WATER LAST

If you didn't think of Whyte's solution, you're in good company. The average person rarely thinks of changing the physical world as a way of changing human behavior. We see that others are misbehaving, and we look to change *them*, not their environment. Caught up in the human side of things, we completely miss the impact of subtle yet powerful sources such as the size of a room or the impact of a chair.

One of our most powerful sources of influence is often the least used because it's the least noticeable. In the words of Fred Steele, the renowned sociotechnical theorist, most of us are "environmentally incompetent."

For example, the authors once met with the president of a large insurance company who lamented that no one gave him tough feed-back. He pointed to recent instances where he had made important decisions with bad information because people were reluctant to chal-lenge his opinions. "I keep telling people to open up, but it's not work-ing," he complained.

The first time we met with him in person we had to traverse six hallways (each the length of an aircraft carrier), walk by hundreds of thousands of dollars of museum-quality artwork, then pass through a security entrance and a formal waiting area. Finally, we entered the president's office to find him seated behind a desk the size of a pickle-ball court. Then, while seated in loosely stuffed chairs that slung us next to the floor and pushed our knees up and into our chests, we stared up at the president, much like grade-school children looking up at the principal.

The president's first words were, "I get the feeling that people around here are scared to talk to me."

Perhaps he had missed the fact that his office was laid out like Hitler's chancellery. (Hitler demanded more than 480 feet of hallway so that visitors would "get a taste of the power and grandeur of the German Reich" on arriving.)[2]

Structural forces have a big impact on behavior, so it's important to spend time discovering them.

## "THINGS" MATTER

Common categories of structural influencers include the physical, informational, virtual, and social. For example, changing a policy, law, or work process can prompt significant changes in behavior. Changing notifications and home page screens on electronic devices can dramatically reduce impulsive thoughts, feelings, and behaviors. And simply strapping an activity measurement device to your wrist can nudge you toward stairs rather than the elevator more often than usual.

Consider the mostly unnoticed effect of *things* on entire communities. Before the arrival of George Kelling, New York subways were a favorite venue for muggers, murderers, and drug dealers. Kelling, a criminologist and originator of the "broken windows theory" of crime,[3] argued that disordered surroundings send out an unspoken but powerful message that encourages antisocial behavior.

"A broken window left in disrepair," Kelling explained, "suggests that no one is in charge and no one cares."

This relatively minor condition promotes more disorderly behavior, including violence. Kelling advised community leaders to start sweating the small stuff. Under his direction, crews began nightly remediation on graffiti, litter, and vandalism. Officials organized crews in the train yard that rolled paint over newly applied graffiti the instant a subway car came in for service.

Over time, a combination of cleanup and prosecution for minor offenses began to make a difference. Surroundings improved, community pride increased, and petty crimes declined. So did violent crime—by 75 percent. Even seemingly innocuous visual cues shape attitudes and behavior in significant ways.

One final example should suffice to demonstrate how unconscious we can be of environmental influences on our choices. Social scientist Brian Wansink suggests that you and I make over 200 eating decisions every day without realizing it. This mindless eating adds hundreds of calories to our diets without adding at all to our satisfaction.[4]

For example, in partnership with him we once invited a couple of dozen kids from a soccer team to join us for lunch after training vigorously for two hours on a Saturday morning. Half of the kids were randomly assigned to eat on seven-inch diameter plates. The rest used plates roughly twice as large. Then we stealthily measured how much each athlete ate by weighing serving bowls before and after the meal. As you'd expect, the kids with the bigger plates ate more.

What's shocking is *how much* more.

While all the kids reported they had eaten all they wanted, we found that those with the larger plates ate 73 percent more!

Why did some kids eat 73 percent more than equally hungry peers?

Wansink's research has identified dozens of ways that distance, size, color, and placement dramatically affect consumption patterns, but most of us don't take these variables into account when trying to change our own eating habits.

## Why We Overlook the Power of "Things"

Why don't we capitalize on the influence of *things* as much as we could? There are two reasons:

1. **Invisibility.** Elements from our environment remain invisible to us. Work procedures, office layouts, and reporting structures aren't always obvious culprits, and we often fail to notice their impact.

2. **Incompetence.** Even when we do think about the impact of our environment, we don't know what to do about it. It's not as if we're carrying around a head full of sociophysical theories. If someone were to tell us that we need to worry about Festinger, Schachter, and Lewin's theory of propinquity (the impact of space on relationships—a topic we'll explore later), we'd think he or she was pulling our leg. Propinquity? Who's ever heard of propinquity?

To access this last, crucial set of influence tools, we must become environmentally competent. We must (1) remember to think about *things* and (2) be able to come up with theories of how changing *things* will change behavior.

There are too many structural influence factors in the world to address in one chapter. So rather than attempt a comprehensive treatment of everything that enables or inhibits behavior, we'll call attention to a few that are most often overlooked or underestimated.

We hope these illustrations prompt you to look carefully at the structural factors that might be of greatest significance to you as a leader.

### Learn to Use "Things" to Make Good Behavior Easier

One of the simplest ways to increase your influence is to make physical and virtual changes that make bad behavior harder and good behavior easier. We'll discuss five ways of achieving this:

1. Add a cue.
2. Change the data stream.
3. Promote propinquity.
4. Make it easy.
5. Change a process.

## ADD A CUE

When behavior is unconscious—as so much of our behavior is—a simple cue can help people make more conscious, better choices.

For example, in another experiment, Brian Wansink gave cans of stacked potato chips to various subjects.[5] Control subjects were given normal cans with uniform chips piled one on top of the other. Experimental subjects were given cans in which every tenth chip was an odd color. The next nine chips would be normal and were followed by another odd-colored chip.

Subjects were asked to engage in other activities while snacking on their chips. Afterward, researchers measured how much each subject had consumed. Those with the colored chips consumed 37 percent less than control subjects who had no indication of how many chips they'd eaten.

What was going on here? By coloring every tenth chip, Wansink helped make the invisible visible. Nobody said anything about the chips or the colors. Nobody encouraged people to control their eating. But the visual cue made eaters conscious of the volume of chips they were eating, and that awareness alone helped them make a decision rather than follow an impulse.

Using cues to make the invisible visible offers potent influence in the workplace as well. In the 1960s, Emery Air Freight pioneered the use of containerized shipping.[6] The company came up with the idea of using sturdy, reusable, and uniformly sized containers—and the whole world changed.

Uniform containers were so much more efficient than previous methods that international shipping prices plummeted. Along with the unprecedented drop in price, industries that had previously been protected from global competition because of high transportation costs (e.g., steel and automobiles) suddenly found themselves competing with anyone, anywhere.

And yet, early on, Edward Feeney, Emery's vice president of systems performance at the time, was frustrated because he couldn't get the workforce to use the new containers to their capacity. Containers were being sealed and shipped without being properly filled. An audit team found they were being properly filled only 45 percent of the time. The workers were extensively trained and constantly reminded of the importance of completely filling the containers, but they were still failing to do it more than half of the time.

After exhausting attempts to influence better behaviors, Feeney stumbled on a method that worked instantly. He simply drew a "fill to here" line on the inside of every container.

Immediately, the rate of completely filled containers went from 45 percent to 95 percent. All it took was a small cue that made the invisible visible.

A hospital we worked with achieved dramatic cost savings with a similarly simple cue. Leaders encouraged clinicians to pay attention to even small product decisions that eventually cost a great deal of money. For example, a type of powderless latex gloves cost over 10 times more than a pair of regular, less-comfortable disposable gloves. Yet in spite of regular pleas from senior management to reduce costs, almost everyone in the facility continued to use the pricey gloves for even short tasks.

The powderless latex was more comfortable than the cheaper gloves, and besides, what were a few pennies here and there?

Then one day someone placed a "25¢" sign on the box of inexpensive gloves and a "$3.00" sign on the box of pricier latex gloves. Problem solved. Once fuller information was made visible, people made more deliberate choices and the use of the expensive gloves dropped dramatically.

### Act Like an Influencer

In the mid-1990s, Bogotá, Colombia, faced a terrible water shortage. Mayor Antanas Mockus rallied various sources of influence to reduce water use by 40 percent in a matter of months. One of his strategies involved a cue to help people hear his message loud and clear.

After airing public service announcements in which he taught water-saving vital behaviors, he used the country's overloaded phone system to cleverly cue people to practice the behaviors. Every time they got a busy signal, rather than hearing a tedious, rhythmic beep, they got either Mockus's voice or that of the Colombian pop star Shakira saying, "Thank you for saving water!"[7]

## CHANGE THE DATA STREAM

The leaders we just cited had one strategy in common: they showcased select information at crucial moments to prompt different decisions. In these cases, individuals weren't resisting better choices because of a bad attitude. Their behavior was shaped by their data stream. The gloves they chose or the level to which they filled a container was driven by the information—or lack thereof—in their immediate experience. Merely tweaking their data stream was sufficient to change behavior.

Despite the fact that we're often exposed to incomplete or inaccurate data, if information is fed to us frequently and routinely enough, we begin to act on it as if it were an accurate sample of the greater reality, even when it often isn't. For example, try this experiment. As quickly as you can, name every place in the world where armed conflict is currently taking place. If you're like most people, you can name an average of two to four places. Now ask yourself why you named these particular locales. Is it because these are the only places? Perhaps they're locations where there is the most bloodshed? Or is it because these are the places of most political significance?

It's probably because these are the sites that have received sustained media coverage. At any one time there are as many as two dozen armed conflicts taking place throughout the world, and it's not uncommon that some of the most horrific battles go largely unnoticed by the international audience. What's shocking about this is *not* that our mental agenda is so heavily influenced by a handful of news producers. It's that we are typically unaware that it's happening.

Influential leaders understand the importance of an accurate data stream and serving up visible, timely, and accurate information that supports their goals. Instead of falling victim to data, they manage it.

Imagine what Dr. Donald Hopkins at The Carter Center was up against when he kicked off the global campaign to eradicate Guinea worm disease. His biggest challenge was to move it to the top of the agenda of developing-world leaders who typically worried a lot more about coups, economic disasters, and corrupt politicians than about parasites.

Add to competing priorities the fact that most leaders had grown up in urban areas and were completely unaware of the pervasive effects of the Guinea worm in their own country.

Jimmy Carter, former US president and founder of The Carter Center, told us that the first challenge leaders faced when attacking

Guinea worm disease in Pakistan was that the president of Pakistan had never even heard of the parasite. Even leaders who knew how widespread the problem was paid little attention to the villages that were plagued because they drew their political support from urban areas.

Dr. Donald Hopkins saved millions from a dreaded disease
without even finding a cure.

Dr. Hopkins addressed this problem by presenting data in clever ways to influence the priorities of heads of state. In Nigeria, for example, national leaders assumed that there were only a few thousand cases nationwide. In 1989, after village coordinators from around the country reported the number of infections in their region, leaders were horrified to discover that there were well over 650,000 cases. They had been off by 3,000 percent! This made Nigeria the most endemic country in the world.

With that new piece of information alone, support for eradicating the disease skyrocketed.

Dr. Hopkins gets the information in front of leaders in a way that gets their attention. His team publishes lots of graphs, charts, and tables. But none has been more influential than the Guinea worm race. Remember the graphic of a racetrack with the faces of the heads of state showing where they were in the race to eradicate the disease?

"I was talking with the president of Burkina Faso," Hopkins reports, "and sharing some concerns about the campaign. I had all kinds of graphs and charts, but the one he wanted to look at the most was the Guinea worm race. They can't stand to be at the bottom. It gets their attention."

There's nothing like a little bit of data coupled with a social nudge to both motivate and enable change.

At the corporate level, the fact that different groups of employees are exposed to wildly different data streams helps explain why people often have such different priorities and passions.

The frontline employees who interface with complaining customers usually become the customer advocates. The top-level executives who are constantly poring over financial statements become the shareholder advocates. And those who routinely take quality measures become the quality advocates.

It's hard to expect people to act in balanced ways when they have access to only one data stream.

For instance, members of a group of senior executives we worked with were driven by their production numbers, which they reviewed weekly. When issues of morale came up (usually with the issuance of a grievance), they'd become rightfully concerned about "people problems," but generally only after it was too late. The same was true for customer satisfaction. This was also listed as a high priority, but nobody ever actually talked about customers or did anything to improve customer relationships until the company lost a major client to a competitor.

To change the executives' narrow focus, we changed the data stream. Alongside weekly production numbers, executives now enthusiastically pore over customer and employee data. Now they spread their attention across more stakeholders.

We also provided employees who had long shown passion for customer satisfaction with weekly cost and profit data, and they too broadened their interests. When faced with a dissatisfied customer, instead of simply throwing money at the problem (often the easiest solution), employees began to seek other, more cost-effective fixes.

Before the intervention, both leaders and employees talked about the importance of all their stakeholders. But nothing changed their behavior until their data stream expanded.

One warning about data. When it comes to data, there is such a thing as "too much of a good thing." An incessant flow of reports, dashboards, and emails transforms into numbing and incoherent background noise. Great leaders avoid this mistake. They're focused and deliberate about the data they share. They understand that the only reason for gathering or publishing data is to reinforce vital behaviors.

## Act Like an Influencer

The leaders of a condo association were frustrated with the money they were spending maintaining trees. Every year 50 or more trees died and were replaced at about $500 per tree. As far as the property management was concerned, the process was automatic. After all, a tree is a tree is a tree—right? Then an owner decided to number and tag each tree and to maintain a database. He tagged about 400 trees and added the species of the tree and the problems it faced.

The association quickly discovered that not all trees are alike and not every tree was suited for every part of their property. In fact, there was one area, a swampy one, where none of the trees they'd planted had survived. And yet they'd faithfully replanted there every year, not taking into consideration which trees would thrive in the wet soil. Creating this simple database influenced people's actions in ways that saved trees, money, and labor.

## PROMOTE PROPINQUITY

In the workplace, one of the most powerful predictors of relationships is the physical environment in which people work. The placement of walls, cubicles, and conference rooms affects who knows whom and who likes whom as much as any other influence. Yet few of us examine these elements when we're trying to understand and change behaviors. Architects create space, and then we live with its effects, mostly unnoticed.

When social psychologist Leon Festinger and others first started examining the effects of space on relationships, they had no idea that they had stumbled onto one of the most profound social-psychological phenomena of all time: propinquity. Simply put, *propinquity* is physical proximity.

For instance, look at who collaborates on spontaneous group efforts at work. Examine who has the most friends and acquaintances in an apartment complex. Explore which employees are satisfied with their relationship with their supervisor. Surely most of these complicated interpersonal scenarios are largely a function of personal interests and interpersonal chemistry—right?

Not really. Festinger discovered that the frequency and quality of human interaction is largely a function of physical distance.[8] Apartment dwellers who are located near stairwells are acquainted with more people than individuals who have fewer people walking by their front doors. And those who live across from the mailboxes know more of their neighbors than anyone else in the building.

At the corporate level, bosses who interact the most frequently with their subordinates generally have the best relationships. And who interacts most often? Bosses who are located closest to their direct reports.

In a study conducted at Bell Labs, researchers tested for factors that determine whether two scientists might collaborate.[9] The best predictor was, you guessed it, *the distance between their offices.* Scientists who worked next to one another were three times more likely to discuss technical topics that led to collaboration than scientists who sat 30 feet from one another. Moving them 90 feet apart lowers the likelihood of collaboration to that of those who work several miles apart! The probability of collaboration sharply decreases in a matter of a few feet.

## What About Virtual Environments?

This might sound like a troubling indictment of the move toward remote and virtual workforces. But our research suggests that propinquity can be achieved through virtual proximity as much as physical. The old model of colocation, where companies demanded that everyone arrive at the same time to the same location, eat lunch on the same schedule, use the same restrooms, and park in the same lot had the happy effect of creating "predictable spontaneity." Employees would connect, share, and build trust through serendipitous interaction. This led many to falsely conclude that colocation was an essential condition for deep employee connection and engagement.

But it never was. If you coax a dozen people into an elevator, they can't help but bump up against each other. But that doesn't mean they'll exit the elevator with a collective determination to excel. If colocation was the key to connection, all colocated organizations would have equally healthy cultures. But they don't. Why? The difference is leadership.

We studied a few hundred organizations that had abruptly shifted from colocation to work-from-home. The majority of those we studied that had made the shift lost an enormous amount of what scholars call *social capital* in the transition. For example, measures of trust, commitment, and discretionary effort (a willingness to give more than the minimum expected) had all plummeted during the two years since the shift had occurred.

The majority had weakened—but not all. About one in four of those we studied was a *positive deviant*. These surprisingly successful organizations had seen dramatic *improvement* in social capital during the exact same transition. Why?

In every case, leaders had created new virtual rituals to replace physical serendipity. They created new norms of virtual socializing, problem-solving, and ad hoc connection that replaced the water cooler, lunchroom, and elevator.

For example, one leader required everyone in her organization to do a "15-minute check-in" every day with an assigned "talking partner." A lightly structured agenda made room for participants to discuss personal life as well as work-related hopes, fears, and successes. Talking partners rotated monthly, giving employees a chance to create meaningful connections with more people.

Examples of social capital–building rituals varied widely in our study, but every organization that had benefited from the transition was the same in one respect: *leaders created virtual structure to replace the physical structure.* They invented intentional practices that enabled a greater sense of connection than their employees experienced in colocation. Geography is not destiny. But leadership is.

When leaders fail to foster social propinquity, whether in colocated or distributed workforces, bad things happen. Silos form and infighting reigns. Employees start labeling others with ugly terms such as "them" and "they"—meaning the bad people "out there" with whom they rarely interact. If you want to predict who doesn't trust or get along with whom in a company, examine propinquity.

## An Example from The Other Side Academy

The Other Side Academy sets the standard for using propinquity to influence change. Dave Durocher's goal, remember, is to foster two vital behaviors. He wants students to be responsible for others rather than just themselves, and he wants to ensure that everyone confronts everyone with whom they have concerns. But how? When they first arrive, these are people who are more likely to punch each other out than lift each other up.

The first thing Durocher does is to stack previously mortal enemies on top of one another. He takes three guys—one new resident who's a card-carrying member of the Mexican Mafia, another who six months earlier was a Crip, and another who just a year ago was a leader in the Aryan Brotherhood—and makes them roommates. Eight such diverse folks might share a dorm. Someone from another background will be the crew boss. It's like a cultural salad bar with every possible grouping tossed into the mix, and then they're asked to help and confront each other—in healthy ways.

We saw the effects firsthand. A fairly new student we'll call Kurt—a white man embroidered with racist prison tattoos—rounded a corner too sharply and nicked a wall with an armoire. Kurt had been at the Academy for just a couple of months and had recently been asked by Andrew, a crew boss, who was Black, to help for the first time in the moving company. Apparently, Kurt hadn't mastered the job yet. What followed was in no small part influenced by the fact that Kurt slept on a bunk four feet above Andrew's—a proximity that had already begun to lower the walls that had previously separated them.

Kurt had come from a majority Black area of Compton, California, where he had been schooled since age six in the hateful propaganda of the white-gang culture. He had been homeless for five years before joining the Academy, and for the first 60 days after entering the program he thought he'd die as his body adjusted to a life without drugs. Taking tight corners with expensive furniture was not his priority.

When Kurt nicked the wall, he ducked his head in shame. The man on the other end of the armoire saw the nick and shook his head in disappointment. Kurt burned with humiliation and began to think seriously about running out the front door. Seeing this, Andrew waited until Kurt finished the maneuver, tugged him by the arm to a quiet corner of the room, and said, "That's the smallest nick a freshman has ever made. I'll go make it right with the customer. Just help me finish this move." Kurt expected many things from Andrew, but not this. An unexpected moment of grace in a vulnerable moment so contradicted the scripts he carried that something inside Kurt shifted. He squared his shoulders and ran back to the truck for his next item.

While there's a lot going on at The Other Side Academy to influence change, you can't help but notice the influence of propinquity. When you make people interdependent and put them in close proximity, you increase the chance that relationships will form and become a big part of their personal transformation.

Families are also affected by how they make use of their environment. For example, a recent study showed that the family dining table is vanishing from homes at a rapid rate. A parallel rise in family dysfunction and discontent suggests that familial unity is declining at a similar rate. Could there be a correlation here? The idea is not that a drop in furniture sales will harm family solidarity. It's that a regular ritual of family dining can facilitate connection. But why would families stop buying and using dining room tables? Behold the microwave. There was a time when the preparation of the evening meal was such a complex undertaking that everyone, of necessity, ate at the same time and in the same place. The microwave changed all that by making it easy to prepare single portions for whomever whenever. Suddenly there was no need to prepare one big meal at one time.

The family dinner was a regular ritual that brought people into face-to-face communication. Nowadays family schedules and structures are far more diverse. Because of that the need for structured opportunities to build connection is even greater and more challenging. Couple the shift away from family meals with the rise of individually consumed media (we watch our personal devices rather than gather around a television), and you'll see how disruptions in structural enablers (source 6) have weakened family ties.

## Propinquity and Rising from Poverty

Great leaders like Bangladesh's Muhammad Yunus leverage propinquity to change lives. For generations Bengali women had been kept from venturing very far outside their own homes. Yunus realized early on that a new environment could provide a context within which impoverished women could slowly and safely invent a new reality. He built inexpensive village bank centers where women would meet in solidarity. A typical meeting is about much more than plotting a business launch or repaying a loan.

We once watched the power of propinquity at the humble village bank building in Gazipur, Bangladesh. One of the tenured women in the group of 30 borrowers walked confidently to the front of the room and greeted her sisters with a snappy two-fingered salute. At once, they stood and recited their "16 Decisions." They fervently and unitedly committed to discipline, unity, courage, and hard work. They pledge that they would no longer live in dilapidated houses. They would grow and eat vegetables. We were tracking pretty well until they got to number 11—"We shall not take dowry at our sons' weddings, neither shall we give any dowry at our daughters' weddings."

Upon asking, we were told that this commitment is of grave importance to the group's economic well-being. The dowry—which parents are required to pay a man to marry their daughter—can cause both social strife and economic disaster. Families are brought to poverty as they try to scrape together enough money for an acceptable dowry. Daughters are routinely berated by fathers who lament the fact that they fathered a girl who would later cost them so much money. Now, here stood 30 women at attention, loudly proclaiming their commitment to abolish the "curse of the dowry."

Later, as we chatted with the 30 women, we asked, "How many of you have had a son or daughter marry in the past year?" Five women proudly raised their hands. And then we sprung the follow-up question. "How many of you either gave or received dowry?" Three hands went sheepishly into the air. But two—Dipali and Shirina—didn't raise theirs. Here was evidence that this millennium-old practice was giving way. So we asked the two women to tell us how they had resisted the practice. They smiled broadly, looked at each other, and then Dipali said, "My son married her daughter." With that the 30 women broke into spontaneous applause.

No longer did these women hide behind their own front doors and simply take what fate handed them. Now they met, talked, formed businesses, supported each other, signed for each other's loans, and became a genuine community, *all within the confines of their own building*. Great leaders leverage the power of propinquity.

### Act Like an Influencer

The senior leaders of a healthcare system were very proud of their new facility, built by a famous architect. Clinical managers disappointed with their poor hand-hygiene numbers suggested adding hand sanitizers inside and outside every door. It was a good idea, but the architect said it would "interrupt the visual flow" of the hallways.

After some discussion, the senior team decided that "bacteria flow is more important than visual flow." Their decision was the right one. Altering this aspect of their physical environment was an important ingredient in bringing their hand-hygiene numbers above 90 percent.

## MAKE IT EASY

The general principle in source 6 is to make it easier to do the right thing and harder to do the wrong thing. Cueing makes it easier to think about making a better decision. Managing the data stream can make it easier to feel differently about various choices. And propinquity does a little of both. Our next strategy involves simply making the behavior itself easier to do. It is easier to motivate someone to do something if it requires little effort to do it.

Effective leaders apply efficiency principles at the very highest level. Rather than constantly finding ways to motivate people to continue with their boring, painful, dangerous, or otherwise unappealing activities, they find a way to change *things*. Skilled leaders change *things* in order to make the right behaviors easier to adopt. They also use *things* to make the wrong behaviors more difficult.

For example, one of the main reasons the Guinea worm disease was eradicated so effectively across the sprawling subcontinent of India was that leaders took steps to make it far easier to drink good water than to drink bad water.

As we saw earlier, leaders from The Carter Center found that villagers who filtered the water had decreased Guinea worm infections. That worked well for those who consumed water carried home from local water supplies. But medical experts discovered that the Guinea worm was often perpetuating itself through occasional drinks taken from distant ponds by itinerant shepherds.

A thirsty boy watching a few goats would happen upon an infected puddle, squat for a sip of water, and ingest invisible larvae. Once infected, if he ventured back to the village's water source, he reintroduced Guinea worm eggs there, giving the worm another year to wreak havoc on the whole community. To solve this problem, Dr. Hopkins and his team could have attempted more aggressive enforcement, more motivational appeals, or even more social pressure. But they didn't. Instead, they created a tool.

They manufactured an inexpensive plastic pipe with a built-in filter that could be used to take a quick drink from available water. The pipe was attractive to shepherds because it offered the added benefit of filtering out more obvious debris and required less bending over to reach the water.

A cheap plastic tool eliminated reintroduction of Guinea worm
to hundreds of villages simply by making a better choice a lot easier to do.

## Back to Propinquity

We've already talked about the power of propinquity. Sometimes just a little *more* distance makes the bad behavior hard enough that it's easier to overcome. For example, in another collaboration with Brian Wansink, we placed bowls filled with colorful M&Ms in 50 of our colleagues' offices. At the end of every day we returned to measure how many had disappeared. In half of the offices the bowls were placed next to the computer keyboard. In the rest, they were placed four feet farther away on the bookshelf. We found that those who had to reach more than an arm's distance ate only half as much.

Simply altering distance can be enough to influence dramatic behavior change. Move your exercise bike from near your TV to your basement, and you've just dramatically cut your chances of using it. Travel to a gym for your routine cardiovascular exercise (as opposed to using a piece of home equipment), and this too might lessen your chances substantially.

*Watch a short video where author Joseph Grenny*
*shares four ways leaders can become*
*more influential at CrucialInfluence.com.*

So, if you're trying to influence your own lifestyle habits, do a quick inventory of things that affect your behavior. Take a count of how many bad food choices are within your reach at each hour of a typical day. Then take a count of how many good choices are within the same distance. Look at how difficult it is for you to exercise. Do you have to walk to a distant and socially isolated room to get to your equipment? Do you have to unpack something from a closet before you can get started? Discover how many items in your home you can simply *move* to make the right behavior easier and the wrong behavior more difficult.

Healthcare institutions have also learned the importance of making the correct behavior easier. Consider what many institutions are doing to reduce medication errors. In the past, pills came only in reddish-brown bottles that offered no information about their content and looked just like the reddish-brown bottles next to them. Couple this challenge with the fact that many people who fill medical orders do so after pulling back-to-back shifts while squinting to read poor handwriting that passes as a prescription, and it's easy to see why medication errors cause tens of thousands of deaths annually.[10]

Nowadays progressive pharmaceutical companies and hospitals make the right choices obvious. By deft use of colored bottles and better labels, many hospitals have significantly reduced medication errors and subsequently needless deaths.

No one knows the wisdom of making choices easier better than the retail world. Consumer guru Paco Underhill helped increase the sales of doggie treats by making it just a little easier to take them off a shelf.[11] Underhill found that young and middle-aged adults were more likely to buy animal treats than were older adults and children. This piqued his curiosity. He videotaped customers in the pet aisle and quickly discovered what was keeping treat sales low among certain age groups. Typically the staple items like pet food were on the eye- and waist-level shelves, while treats were placed on higher shelves.

It turns out that the young and old find it significantly more difficult to reach items on a higher shelf. One video clip showed an older woman attempting to use a carton of aluminum foil to knock down a package of treats. Another revealed a child dangerously climbing shelves to try to reach the package. Moving the treats down one shelf made the behavior just easy enough to boost sales immediately. Love it or hate it, people who want something from you tweak your environment every way they can to part you from your hard-earned money!

## Make It Inevitable

The ultimate way to make better choices easier is to make them inevitable. This is where structure, process, and procedures come into play. Engineers, tired of reminding employees not to stick their fingers in certain machines, build in mechanical features that prevent people from putting their hands at risk. Pilots follow lockstep procedures and rigid checklists that require them to double and triple check their take-off and landing procedures.

When taking orders in the fast-food industry, employees can simply push picture buttons. And of course, nobody has to know how to make change because the register does it automatically.

It's all been routinized so it's now almost impossible to do the wrong thing.

Often all that's required to make good behavior inevitable is to structure it into your daily routine. If we've learned only one thing about today's overscheduled world, it's that structure drives out lack of structure. Meetings happen. On the other hand, "I'll get back to you sometime later"—maybe that won't happen. So, if you want to guarantee a positive behavior, build it into a special meeting or hardwire it into an existing meeting agenda.

For example, one CEO saw a massive increase in innovative breakthroughs when he and his senior leadership team scheduled and met regularly with groups of employees to solicit ideas. This calendared practice created a forum that encouraged and enabled new behaviors, thereby making the right behavior inevitable.

At The Other Side Academy, vital behaviors are hardwired into regular *rituals*. These ordered procedures consist of fixed meetings that are never missed and that are highly symbolic, quite volatile, and enormously effective at making the right behavior inevitable. As we mentioned earlier, one of them is called "Games." This particular ritual is not always fun, but it's always done.

Say you're a student at the Academy. Twice a week you and members of your assigned group get together to give each other unvarnished feedback. Two older students ensure that nothing gets physical, but beyond that it's pretty unstructured. During Games, people learn the unrestricted approach to feedback that The Other Side Academy wants. Anyone can challenge anyone. If you think your crew boss is a jerk, you give him a slip of paper inviting him to a Game. He must show up. And when he's there, you can unload on him to your heart's content. Anyone from Dave Durocher on down can be invited to a Game by anyone else.

Over time, the quality of the Games increases as the volume decreases. Students become better at sharing feedback. What doesn't change is that this long-standing ritual makes the right behavior inevitable. Most people don't like to confront others—particularly scary and powerful others. Left to their own proclivities, students would do what anyone else would do: toggle from silence (holding our complaints inside) to violence (blowing up in a verbal tirade—or worse). So Durocher turns feedback into a ritual, calls it "Games," and then lets the Games begin. Twice a week without fail.

## CHANGE A PROCESS

Most of our behavior is not a product of conscious deliberation. Most follows the structure of habit or routine. For example, you probably bathe in a predictable way—soaping up various body parts in the same order most every time. We have morning rituals, bedtime rituals, and work rituals that gently dictate how we approach most of our recurring activities.

Similarly, the way you run meetings, make group decisions, interview job candidates, and so forth probably follows a process—either tacitly or explicitly. In organizations we call these routines *processes*. No organization would ever achieve any level of efficiency and coordination if groups did not evolve processes for getting things done.

Sometimes the easiest way to lead change is to change a process, routine, or ritual. Simply embedding a vital behavior into an existing process can dramatically change outcomes. For example, years ago we found that medical errors are often the consequence of silence. Altogether too often a surgeon might be preparing to close a patient when a nurse notices that the clamp count is off. In other words, the surgeon might have left something inside the patient that could cause problems later. Our study found that far too often the nurse and others on the team say nothing in these crucial moments.[12] Fortunately, in the years since that study was published, great efforts have been taken to influence change. One surprisingly effective intervention involves simply adding one step to the medical procedure: asking the members of the team to introduce themselves! This little process tweak strengthens psychological safety and pulls each team member out of anonymity, which increases the likelihood that team members will catch and call out potential errors.[13] In addition, research shows that following a checklist significantly improves outcomes and reduces errors.[14] Now, let's be clear, there's a big difference between announcing a checklist and influencing all of your surgical teams to use it! That's where other sources of influence come into play. But structuring a new behavior into a process is a potent part of the influence effort.

Consistent outcomes typically come from consistent behavior. And consistent behavior is often guided by the processes we follow. So, if you don't like your outcomes, take a look at your processes. For example, decades ago, symphony orchestras began to confront the tremendous gender inequity among their musicians. Not only were they hiring men at much higher rates than women, but the men had exclusive hold on coveted leadership positions. Many excused the inequity by claiming the results were the inevitable outcome of a merit-based audition process. Expert judges listened objectively to competing performers, they argued, and the results were the results. This logic held until a number of orchestras tried a new process. They instituted "blind" auditions in which the candidate performed behind a screen, hidden from view. This practice immediately led to a 30 percent increase in female new hires.[15] Changing the process kept the focus solely on factors that should influence the final decision and removed those that shouldn't.

In our home lives, processes take the form of rituals. Rituals are often unconscious—we simply evolve a habit for carrying out recurring tasks. If you're trying to improve some result in your personal life, finding a daily ritual you can attach a new activity to can accelerate change over trying to treat it as a stand-alone task. For example, a friend dramatically improved feelings of warmth and connection in his home by adding one simple step to his "coming home" ritual. That ritual used to involve driving home from the office in stressful traffic, ruminating over everything that had gone wrong at work, then rushing into the house distracted and tense. That emotional noise usually set the tone for his first encounter with his family. To change this, he placed a sticker of a cloud on his steering wheel that reminded him to add a key step to his "coming home" ritual: after parking his car, he took himself through a two-minute meditation that helped him transition from work to family.

The new procedure helped him walk into his home more calm, grateful, and present.

A good influence plan should consider relevant processes and policies that make vital behaviors harder or negative behaviors easier. Sometimes eliminating steps, simplifying decision-making, or delegating authority can dramatically change behavior. Changing processes can have a big impact on helping people behave in ways that improve results and align with their values.

## SUMMARY: STRUCTURAL ABILITY

Many of us are environmentally incompetent—we fail to recognize the subtle but powerful pull of our physical and virtual environments on our behaviors. Given that *things* are far easier to change than *people* and that these things can have a permanent impact on how people behave, it's high time we pick up on the lead of Whyte, Steele, Wansink, and others and add the power of the space we inhabit to our influence repertoire.

1. **Add a cue.** Use cues to prompt attention at the moment a new behavior is needed.
2. **Change the data stream.** Influence hearts and minds by exposing people to information that helps them see what happens when vital behaviors are and are not practiced.
3. **Promote propinquity.** Use distance to shape choices.
4. **Make it easy.** Do all you can to make the behavior reasonably easy and obvious.
5. **Change a process.** Where possible, build the new behavior into policies and processes.

When you get source 6 on your side, you gain a sleepless ally to influence change for good.

# 9

# BECOME A LEADER

*The greatest hope for solving every significant problem we face*
*as a planet is for more people to become influential leaders.*

This book started with a bold assertion. We claimed that if you bundle the right number and type of influences into a robust influence strategy, you can create rapid, profound, and lasting change. We shared research that suggests you can amplify your influence tenfold if you follow the principles practiced by effective leaders around the world. And finally, we offered not just to help you *do* a few things better, we held out hope that *Crucial Influence* skills would improve the way you *think* about every influence challenge you face.

The next time you struggle to find a way to influence change, we hope you'll default to using *the three keys to influence.* Simply ponder and answer the crucial questions:

1. What *result* do I want? And how will I measure progress?
2. What *vital behaviors* are key to achieving that result?

**3.** How do I enlist a critical mass of the *six sources of influence* to support the vital behaviors?

With these crucial questions at the top of your mind, your confidence in facing influence problems should increase. You know the basic building blocks you'll need to assemble an effective strategy.

You now also know how to think about the full variety of influences behind every behavior that concerns you.

First, you'll diagnose your vital behaviors by examining each of the *six sources of influence.*

Next, you'll determine which sources are getting in the way of change by asking questions like those shown.

|  | MOTIVATION | ABILITY |
|---|---|---|
| **PERSONAL** | **1** <br><br> Is it pleasurable or meaningful? | **2** <br><br> Can they do it? |
| **SOCIAL** | **3** <br><br> Are they encouraged to do it? | **4** <br><br> Are they enabled to do it? |
| **STRUCTURAL** | **5** <br><br> Are they rewarded for doing it, or punished for not doing it? | **6** <br><br> Does their environment (both physical and virtual) enable it? |

Questions for the Six Sources of Influence

The magnitude of your influence depends on the quality of your diagnosis. As you carefully study all of the factors that impede change, you'll be more likely to create an influence strategy that promotes change.

Finally, you'll use the tactics you've learned in each chapter to assemble enough of the six sources to make change the path of least resistance. You now know how to *overdetermine* change.

## A POWERFUL MULTIPURPOSE TOOL

There's nothing more empowering than a multipurpose tool. In the three key questions and the Six Sources of Influence, you have a tool robust enough to help you think about everything from your fitness goals to customer retention worries to your water-balloon-throwing teen. And as we'll see in the next example, if you happen to leave this book lying around your home, it might even help your college-age son get his fraternity brothers to open their wallets.

College freshman Daniel Nix had a clear desired result in mind as he approached the end of his first semester: raise $300 from his university Greek house to decorate for the holidays. Daniel adores the holidays and wanted to make his first Christmas away from home cheery. Full of youthful optimism, he set a five-gallon bucket in the house's cafeteria and labeled it "Christmas Light Donations." Then he waited for the money to flow. Three days later he had a grand total of $20 and a gum wrapper in the bucket.

On a visit home he happened across his dad's copy of this book. He spent the weekend devouring it, then confronted his problem with optimism borne of a new way of thinking.

Reading the book didn't change his desired result. $300 was the goal. Nor did it take a lot of thought to decide how to measure progress or identify a vital behavior: he wanted his housemates to cough up cash—electronically or physically.

The breakthrough came as he examined his problem through all six sources of influence and did his best to craft an idea or two from each. Among other things, he decorated the five-gallon bucket in Christmas glory in order to make the pitch easier to see, and to connect to emotions that would promote participation (sources 1 and 6). He posted an enormous picture of Santa's piercing eyes above the bucket, giving the impression that he would know if you were naughty or nice (source 3). He gamified the challenge by displaying a large thermometer displaying progress toward the goal (sources 1 and 6). And he posted the names and donation amounts of everyone who had contributed next to the thermometer (source 3).

Within 48 hours Daniel exceeded his goal. There's nothing more empowering than a multipurpose tool. When you get better at thinking about influence, you get better at leading change.

## A FEW WARNINGS

We'll conclude by sharing two of the most common ways we've seen leaders go wrong when attempting to apply what you now know. These include, ironically, both *overthinking* and *underthinking* influence. Let's take a look at these two traps in turn.

### Overthinking

While we encourage leaders to consider every source of influence as they build an influence plan, not all circumstances require a full six-source campaign.

If you're not up against a great deal of resistance, you may not need to overthink the problem. It could be that simply throwing one or two more sources of influence at the behavior will invite change.

Similarly, if the risk of failure is low, you don't need to conduct an elaborate diagnosis, then deliberate at length about influence options.

Just use the Crucial Influence model to brainstorm some possibilities and see what happens.

For example, one of the authors was able to exercise more consistently by simply putting his exercise clothes and shoes on a chair by his bed (source 6). He suspected that if he immediately dressed for a run when he woke in the morning, he might run more consistently. And it worked. Had it not worked, he wouldn't have lost much in the experiment. He could have stepped back at that point and taken a more serious look at ways of engaging more sources of influence.

If the need for change is neither terribly urgent nor dangerously important, just run a few experiments by tweaking a source of influence or two. It's better in these cases to get started and adjust a couple of times than waste time as you overthink the problem.

## Underthinking

On the flip side of overthinking, sometimes people don't give influence enough thought. You can do this in one of two ways. Ironically, you can make this mistake with either big or small problems. Underthinking also often shows up in the form of *thrifting*.

### Small Problems

Sometimes readers get less than the full value of their investment in this book because they mistakenly conclude that its primary value is for solving big, hairy, overwhelming problems. If "curing a pandemic" isn't on their to-do list for the week, they set what they've learned aside.

Don't make that mistake! Recall the dozens of examples we've shared of deft use of key ideas in-the-moment. These leaders didn't need to solve big problems, but they thought more carefully about even their small problems in ways that made them far more effective. Developing the discipline of considering all of the sources of influence amplifies your leadership with even everyday challenges.

For example, when you're counseling one of your children, watch for your tendency to treat ability problems (sources 2, 4, and 6) as motivation problems. When you're writing a memo that demands action, use a story (source 1) to help people connect with a more motivating moral frame. When you're setting up a room for a meeting, think about how the layout of the room (source 6) will influence behavior. Next time you send people off to training (source 2), consider adding some social influence (sources 3 and 4) by meeting with them before and after to support their action plans.

Don't miss the hundreds of opportunities life presents to you to think and act more intentionally about influence. A little more thought can lead to a lot more influence.

## Thrifting

It's not uncommon when we get to the end of a lecture on the six-source model to have an executive raise their hand and ask something like, "Which source of influence is the most important?" When this question comes up, we panic.

This question betrays a worrisome misunderstanding of the entire message of this book. Our goal has been to give you a proper appreciation of how all the sources of influence shape behavior. To us, asking, "Which is most important?" is like asking, "Which major human organ is most important? Heart? Lungs? Brain? Can you prioritize those for me?"

The Six-Sources of Influence is a model of systemic influence. Each source interacts with others to produce action, and each may affect some people more than others. That's why our overriding message is that if change is important, your goal should be to *overdetermine* success.

But that's not the way things work in most organizations. Because they're used to striving for efficiency, most leaders ask, "What's the least we can do to get results?"

If you begin an influence effort with "thrifting" in mind, you're likely to fail.

Many of the great leaders you've learned about here are familiar with this concern. People make pilgrimages to visit with Martha Swai, Dr. Don Berwick, Dr. Wiwat Rojanapithayakorn, Dave Durocher, and others to learn the secrets to their success. Then rather than look at all of the sources of influence these highly influential leaders have employed, these naive people scrounge for one or two silver bullets to cobble onto their existing efforts in hopes of putting them over the top.

They attach a Ferrari hood ornament to their 1974 Pinto wagon and wait for heads to turn. But they don't. It's still a Pinto.

For example, civic and police leaders have descended on North Carolina to learn about the "Second Chance" strategy we describe in Chapter 7. After studying the strategy's complex system for influencing change, these leadership tourists often focus solely on the made-for-TV meetings where soon-to-be-arrested drug dealers are brought into a room filled with pictures of themselves committing crimes. Surely that is the "most important" part of the influence strategy, right? So they fly back home, identify their most notorious offenders, gather the evidence, produce the video, and host the party. And re-offense rates don't change one iota.

Why? If you think about that question through the framework of the six sources, you'll see that such an approach neglects every other source of influence that is embedded in the Second Chance strategy.

Might you need more than a terrifying confrontation with a district attorney to help someone fundamentally change decades-long criminal behaviors? The North Carolina effort engages not just fear of consequences, but family support (sources 3 and 4), job training (source 2), scholarship incentives (source 5), peer influence (sources 3 and 4), relocation (source 6), and much more.

Designers of the Second Chance program went to great pains to ensure that all six sources of influence are incorporated into their efforts. But "thrifters" want to treat the influence effort like a box of chocolates and simply pick their favorites.

## Diagnose to Overcome Thrifting

Over the years we've found that leaders are less likely to fall prey to thrifting if they've thoroughly diagnosed the problem. If they've gathered data about how well (or poorly) *all* sources of influence are aligned with the behaviors they hope to foster, they create more realistic influence plans.

Dr. Warren Warwick of the University of Minnesota Medical Center in Fairview offered a great example of how good diagnosis leads to effective leadership. Warwick treated patients with cystic fibrosis (CF). CF is a genetic condition that causes the body to produce thick, sticky mucus in places like the lungs or digestive tract that should instead have slippery, flexible protective coatings. Left untreated, sufferers risk compromised breathing and malnutrition as the dense material inhibits functioning of both lungs and digestive tracts. Unfortunately, treatments can be not only inconvenient, but painful. For example, buildup in the lungs might need to be broken down using a process of aggressive massage.

Warwick often faced patients who were failing to practice lifesaving behaviors. Over time, he came to realize that the effectiveness of his medical skills depended on his proficiency at influence. This insight prompted him to develop a discipline of diagnosis—not just of the disease, but of the sources of influence his patients confronted when attempting to follow his advice.

For example, one day Dr. Warwick sat with an 18-year-old CF patient who wasn't conforming to her treatment plan. Rather than launch into a lecture about how she would suffocate in a few years (source 1: an attempt to motivate compliance) if she continued to slack off, Dr. Warwick stopped and diagnosed *all* the underlying causes. As he listened, he gained a humbling appreciation for her lapses.

The patient had a new boyfriend with whom she was staying half the time. Her mother had typically administered treatments, but now the daughter was often not at home at the prescribed times (a loss of sources 3 and 4). The patient had also started a job and was working nights (a source 6 schedule change). The school she attended had changed policies and now required a nurse to administer her medicine (a policy that introduced a source 6 barrier). Deciding that this was a pain, she stopped taking her medicine.

In spite of having lost 20 percent of her lung capacity in the previous two months, she felt fine and concluded that fewer treatments were OK (a possible source 1 motivation for compliance wasn't proving effective).

The more Dr. Warwick listened to the patient, the more he appreciated that her situation was complex, and the less tempted he was to thrift his influence by simply putting the fear of death into her. He and the patient jointly developed a plan to overcome obstacles and literally saved her life.

Good diagnosis leads to effective influence by revealing the humbling complexity of human behavior.

## CONTINUE YOUR LEARNING

We wish you the best in your efforts to become a better leader. As we said in Chapter 1, leadership is intentional influence. It is the systematic process of influencing human behavior to achieve great things. The greatest hope for solving every significant problem we face as a planet is for more people to become influential leaders.

We hope your investment in studying this book produces tremendous returns in your effort to offer positive influence in the world. Whether your efforts improve the quality of your own life, boost your company's success, or bless lives in your community, we applaud you for becoming part of the noble work of those you've met in these pages.

We also hope that the framework we've offered motivates you to *continue* your learning. While we've described potent influence tactics within each of the sources, we have by no means exhausted the ways you can engage any of them. New findings are published every day for how to help people find more personal motivation, exert social influence, and reshape environments to foster positive change. Keep learning!

*Watch a short video where author Joseph Grenny shares how to use your new skills to influence those in your organization. See it at CrucialInfluence.com.*

To help, we invite you to visit CrucialInfluence.com. There you'll find great learning aids, including:

- The Crucial Influence assessment that not only gives you a view into your existing influence strengths and weaknesses but can also help you develop the next steps for becoming an effective influencer
- Discussion questions you can use with your book club or reading group
- The Six Sources of Influence model
- Videos of interviews with some of the leaders you've met in this book
- Case studies of organizations that have used the Crucial Influence model to great success
- A free subscription to the *Crucial Skills* newsletter, a Q&A column that addresses tough interpersonal and organizational challenges

As Margaret Mead once said, "Never doubt that a small group of thoughtful, committed citizens can change the world; indeed, it is the only thing that ever has."

Best wishes in your efforts to become a more thoughtful and effective leader.

# NOTES

## Chapter 1

1. Sedaris, D. (2009). *Naked*. Little, Brown and Company. p. 215.

## Chapter 2

1. Gauggel, S., and Billino, J. (2002). "The Effects of Goal Setting on the Arithmetic Performance of Brain-Damaged Patients." *Archives of Clinical Neuropsychology* 17, no. 3: 283–294, http://www.sciencedirect .com/science/article/pii/S0887617701001135. This German study has shown that even brain-damaged patients perform arithmetic better when they have been given a clear and challenging goal than when they have been given a vague "do your best" challenge. Also see Gellatly, I. R., and Meyer, J. P. (1992). "The Effects of Goal Difficulty on Physiological Arousal, Cognition, and Task Performance." *Journal of Applied Psychology* 77, no. 5: 694–704, https://doi.org/10.1037/ 0021-9010.77.5.694, http://psycnet.apa.org/journals/apl/77/5/694/. This study has shown the presence of a challenging goal has both cognitive and behavioral effects, including heart rate.

2. In previous editions of this book we highlighted the case of Delancey Street Foundation in San Francisco led by Mimi Silbert. The authors were so struck with what she had accomplished, but disappointed with how little replication there had been of the model that in 2015 they funded and led an effort to spur more adoption and innovation. As of the writing of this book, in addition to the flagship campus of The Other Side Academy in Salt Lake City, Utah, there are five other successful campuses with more in the planning stages. Information is available at TheOtherSideAcademy.com.

3. McKane, S. (2021). "The Other Side Academy Helping Former Addicts and Criminals Turn Their Lives Around," Fox 13, Salt Lake City. https://

www.fox13now.com/news/local-news/the-other-side-academy
-helping-former-addicts-and-criminals-turn-their-lives-around.
4. Grenny, J. (2008). "Influencer: The Power to Change Anything." *MIT Sloan Management Review*, 49(2), 60–67.

## Part II

1. Mencken, H. L. (1920). *Prejudices: Second Series*. Alfred A. Knopf. p. 158.

## Chapter 3

1. Haidt, J. (2006). *The Happiness Hypothesis: Finding Modern Truth in Ancient* Wisdom. Basic Books.

## Chapter 4

1. Dweck, C. (2006). *Mindset: The New Psychology of Success*. Random House.
2. Mischel, W., Shoda, Y., and Rodriguez, M. L. (1989). "Delay of Gratification in Children." *Science* 244(4907), 933–938.
3. Bandura, A., and Mischel, W. (1966). "Moral Reasoning and Vicarious Learning." *Journal of Abnormal and Social Psychology* 63(2), 311–318.
4. Ericsson, K. A., Krampe, R. T., and Tesch-Römer, C. (1993). "The Role of Deliberate Practice in the Acquisition of Expert Performance." *Psychological Review*, 100(3), 363–406.
5. Maxfield, D., Grenny, J., McMillan, R., Patterson, K., and Switzler, A. (2005). "Silence Kills: The Seven Crucial Conversations for Healthcare." *Journal of Patient Safety* 1(2), 7–16.

## Chapter 5

1. Milgram, S. (1963). "Behavioral Study of Obedience." *Journal of Abnormal and Social Psychology*, 67(4), 371–378.
2. Maxfield, D., Grenny, J., McMillan, R., Patterson, K., and Switzler, A. (2005). "Silence Kills: The Seven Crucial Conversations for Healthcare." *Journal of Patient Safety* 1(2), 7–16.

## Chapter 6

1. Wansink, B., and Cheney, M. M. (2005). "Super Bowls: Serving Bowl Size and Food Consumption." *JAMA* 293(14), 1727–1728.
2. Gneezy, U., Haruvy, E., and Yafe, H. (2004). "The Inefficiency of Splitting the Bill," *The Economic Journal* 114, no. 495: 265–280, https://doiorg/10.1111/j.1468-0297.2004.00209.x.

3. Bernick, C. L. (2001). "When Your Culture Needs a Makeover." *Harvard Business Review*, 53–61.
4. https://hopesquad.com/mission-history/.

## Chapter 7

1. Sloman, S., and Fernbach, P. (2017) *The Knowledge Illusion: Why We Never Think Alone*. Riverhead Books.
2. Lepper, M. R., Greene, D., and Nisbett, R. E. (1973). "Undermining Children's Intrinsic Interest with Extrinsic Reward: A Test of the 'Overjustification' Hypothesis." *Journal of Personality and Social Psychology* 28(1), 129–137.
3. Higgins, S. T., Budney, A. J., and Bickel, W. K. (1994). "Achieving Cocaine Abstinence with a Behavioral Approach." *Addiction* 89(11), 1541–1548.
4. Masaaki, I. (1986). *Kaizen: The Key to Japan's Competitive Success*. McGraw-Hill.
5. https://ncsecondchance.org/about/.
6. https://www.populationmedia.org/stories/spotlight-dr-negussie-teffera.

## Chapter 8

1. Whyte, W. F. (1948). "Human Relations in the Restaurant Industry." *Harvard Business Review* 26(5), 367–376.
2. Speer, A. (1970). *Inside the Third Reich: Memoirs*. Macmillan.
3. Kelling, G. L., and Coles, C. M. (2006). *Fixing Broken Windows: Restoring Order and Reducing Crime in Our Communities*. Simon and Schuster,.
4. Wansink, B. (2006). *Mindless Eating: Why We Eat More Than We Think*. Bantam Books.
5. Wansink, B. (2004). "Environmental Factors That Increase the Food Intake and Consumption Volume of Unknowing Consumers." *Annual Review of Nutrition* 24(1), 455–479.
6. Levinson, M. (2006). "The Box That Changed the World." *Harvard Business Review* 84(3), 62–77.
7. Hanauer, J. (2001). *Civic Culture and Urban Change: Governing Dallas*. University Press of Kansas. https://www.nytimes.com/2015/07/17/opinion/the-art-of-changing-a-city.html.
8. Festinger, L., Schachter, S., and Back, K. (1950). *Social Pressures in Informal Groups: A Study of Human Factors in Housing*. Harper.
9. Allen, T. J. (1977). "Managing the Flow of Technology: Technology Transfer and the Dissemination of Technological Information within the R&D Organization." *Administrative Science Quarterly* 22(2), 242–263.

10. Makary, M. A., and Daniel, M. (2016). "Medical Error—the Third Leading Cause of Death in the US." *BMJ Quality & Safety* 25(10), 726–732.

11. Underhill, P. (1999). *Why We Buy: The Science of Shopping.* Simon & Schuster.

12. Maxfield, D. G., Grenny, J., McMillan, R., Patterson, K., and Switzler, A. (2005). "Silence Kills: Seven Crucial Conversations in Healthcare." Patient Safety Network. https://psnet.ahrq.gov/issue/silence-kills -seven-crucial-conversations-healthcare.

13. Gawande, A. *The Checklist Manifesto,* A 2008 study for surgical patients in eight hospitals showed that those who used a surgical procedure requiring personal introductions had 36 percent fewer major complications. Deaths fell 47 percent.

14. Haynes A.B., Weiser T.G., Lipsitz S.R., et al. (2009). "A Surgical Safety Checklist to Reduce Morbidity and Mortality in a Global Population." *N Engl J Med.* 360(5): 491–499. https://www.hsph.harvard.edu/news/ features/ellner-surgical-safety-checklist-and-training-lowers -complications/.

15. Goldin, C., and Rouse, C. (2000). "Orchestrating Impartiality: The Impact of 'Blind' Auditions on Female Musicians." *American Economic Review* 90(4), 715–741. https://gap.hks.harvard.edu/orchestrating -impartiality-impact-%E2%80%9Cblind%E2%80%9D-auditions-female -musicians.

# INDEX

# Index

# ABOUT THE AUTHORS

**Joseph Grenny** is an author, speaker, and social scientist for business performance. He has advised leaders on every major continent, from the boardrooms of Fortune 500 companies to the communities in Nairobi, Kenya. He has cofounded three not-for-profit organizations: Unitus Labs, The Other Side Academy, and The Other Side Village.

**Kerry Patterson** (1946–2022) has coauthored four award-winning training programs and led multiple long-term change efforts in Fortune 500 organizations around the world. He is the recipient of the BYU Marriott School of Management Dyer Award for outstanding contribution in organizational behavior. Kerry completed doctoral work at Stanford University.

**David Maxfield** is a leading researcher, consultant, and speaker. He has led research studies on the role of human behavior in medical errors, safety hazards, and project execution. He completed doctoral work in psychology at Stanford University.

**Ron McMillan** is a leading researcher, consultant, and speaker. He has led research studies on the role of human behavior in medical errors, safety hazards, and project execution. He completed doctoral work in psychology at Stanford University.

**Al Switzler** is a renowned consultant who has directed training and management initiatives with leaders from Fortune 500 companies worldwide. He also served on the faculty of the Executive Development center at the University of Michigan.

# LOVE THE BOOKS?
## MEET THE COURSES

# About Crucial Learning

Crucial Learning improves the world by helping people improve themselves. By combining social science research with innovative instructional design, we create flexible learning experiences that teach proven skills for solving life's most stubborn personal, interpersonal, and organizational problems. We offer courses in communication, performance, and leadership, focusing on behaviors that have a disproportionate impact on outcomes, called crucial skills. Our award-winning courses and accompanying bestselling books include *Crucial Conversations, Crucial Accountability, Crucial Influence* (formerly *Influencer*), *The Power of Habit,* and *Getting Things Done.* Together they have helped millions achieve better relationships and results, and nearly half of the Forbes Global 2000 have drawn on these crucial skills to improve organizational health and performance.

CrucialLearning.com

# Also from the Crucial Learning Author Team

"This is a breakthrough book. I found myself being deeply influenced, motivated, and even inspired."

—Stephen R. Covey, author of *The 7 Habits of Highly Effective People*

"If you read only one 'management' book this decade... I'd insist that it be *Crucial Accountability*."

—Tom Peters, author of *In Search of Excellence*

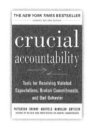

"At Zappos, one of our core values is to 'Embrace and Drive Change.' This book shows how adapting one's life or career for the better can be done in a new and powerful way."

—Tony Hsieh, Former CEO of Zappos.com, Inc.

"Sharp, provocative, and useful."

—Jim Collins, author of *Good to Great*

"I am a devout, card-carrying GTD true believer. The entire approach has boosted not only my productivity but also my wider well-being...GTD has taken hold around the world. This is a genuine movement."

—Daniel Pink, author of *Drive*

# Resources for Book Readers

Ever read a book on yoga and then assumed you'd be able to do astavakrasana? Trust us, it doesn't work. Just like yoga, influence isn't something you master by reading a book. It's something you practice over and over again. And we've made it easier to do so.

The following resources are used in our Crucial Influence course. Now they're free to you. Go to **CrucialInfluence.com** and continue developing your skills.

 **Influence Challenge**
Face a situation where you need to get better results? Use this worksheet to plan your next change initiative.

 **Crucial Influence Assessment**
Discover your natural leadership tendencies and identify where you can improve.

 **Video Library**
Watch interviews with some of the leaders you've read about in this book.

 **Crucial Skills Newsletter**
Subscribe to our Q&A newsletter and send us your tough questions. Each week our authors and experts answer reader questions about how to handle crucial moments.

**Find these resources and more at CrucialInfluence.com.**